THE BIG RED BOOK

Rangers' Robert Malcom pushes through against Celtic's Chris Sutton in the CIS Insurance Cup semi-final

THE BIG RED BOOK

Ronnie Cully and Roy McCormack

In association with

Sponsored by

Black & White Publishing

First published 2001
by Black & White Publishing Ltd
99 Giles Street, Edinburgh EH6 6BZ

ISBN 1 902927 34 6

Photographs on the following pages have been reproduced by kind
permission of EMPICS Ltd: ii, viii, xi, 17, 19, 35, 38, 40, 46, 47, 50, 56, 60, 71, 73,
74, 78, 79, 82, 96, 98, 102, 103, 104, 105, 106, 108, 116, 118, 121

A CIP catalogue record for this book is available from The British Library.

Printed and bound by Scotprint, Haddington

Designed by McCusker Graphic Media

CONTENTS

BANK OF SCOTLAND

PROUD SPONSORS

OF THE

SCOTTISH

PREMIER LEAGUE

FOREWORD

The Wee Red Book has been an institution – a central plank within Scottish football – for as long as I can recall: as a boy starting out in the game, as a player, as a club manager and then coach of Scotland's international team. So the arrival of what you might term its brother, *The Big Red Book*, is more than welcome to all of us who have a profound interest in the former glories and disappointments of the game and, indeed, in its future.

The little guy, *The Wee Red Book*, has never been far from my reach. It has settled nicely in my jacket pocket, on top of my desk, in a drawer or at my home. My first recollection of the publication was as a schoolboy. It was essential reading for any kid interested in Scottish football, and the fascination supporters have always had with statistics carried on for me into the professional game. When I was at Rangers in the late 1950s I can vividly recall looking through its pages. To see your face within the first team group, no matter how tiny it was, became a very special moment. Similarly, every Scottish footballer I have ever known through the years has always carried a copy. Disputes in pubs, clubs, dressing rooms and boardrooms have been settled by the facts laid out in its pages.

So those of us within the game will welcome this addition to a tradition. I am confident it will go on to emulate the success of its predecessor.

Craig Brown
Former Scotland
National Team Coach

Aberdeen's Derek Young battles for the ball with Giovanni van Bronckhorst of Rangers in the third round of the CIS Insurance Cup

INTRODUCTION

Scottish football lined up to face the 21st century certain of its goal, but unsure of its formation. In many cases there were even doubts they could play all the way to the final whistle. Just like in TV soap land, another crossroad had been reached. The rich were getting richer, but still felt unrewarded for their efforts, whilst the poor were trading on goodwill and borrowed time.

As season 2000–1 kicked off, most people with an interest in football – whether as a casual spectator or headline star – agreed our game was on the threshold of change. It had to be for its very survival. A summer of watching from the outside as the Euro 2000 finals were played out in Belgium and Holland without Scotland had not done much to restore morale. At least the Rangers fans could take more than a little comfort from watching their side romp away with the SPL championship, finishing no fewer than 21 points clear of nearest challengers Celtic. However, even that achievement felt like something of a hollow victory for a number of Rangers followers who had by then

Most people agreed our game was on the threshold of change. It had to be for its very survival

lifted their sights to horizons outwith Scotland's boundaries. Europe was the arena in which they wanted to perform regularly and well. Fuelled by the same ambition, manager Dick Advocaat plunged heavily into the transfer market once again, his major purchases at the summer sales being fellow Dutchmen Fernando Ricksen and Bert Konterman.

Across the city it was not new players who were giving rise to fresh hope, it was the arrival of one man — Martin O'Neill. While many warned the amiable Ulsterman of the huge task he faced in getting Celtic back on an even keel, others cautioned him that he had left the security of Leicester City to accept a poisoned chalice.

After the debacle into which the John Barnes/Kenny Dalglish stewardship had degenerated, how could anyone expect to restore the Parkhead club's dignity, let alone their title credentials? The astonishing fall from grace suffered by Celtic in not only conceding the League long before the final whistle, but also falling to Inverness Caley Thistle at home in the

Scottish Cup third round, proved highly embarrassing for the club. Worse still, it was also catastrophic in terms of strangling the competition – the oxygen of the Scottish game. For the game in this country to be vibrant, both halves of the Old Firm need to be offering a viable challenge for the honours. That energy permeates down through the rest of the Scottish Premier League, and indeed into the three lower divisions. There the target is, as ever, survival rather than success.

There are exceptions to the rule, however – nowhere better illustrated than in Livingston, where they have shown what a little bit of money and a lot of ambition can achieve. Even lower down – some may say amongst clubs who have long since ceased to do much more than tread water – a couple of clubs were happy to jump into what was, for them, the deep end of our senior game.

With the SPL increased to 12 clubs in yet another act of self-preservation dressed up as restructuring, the door was finally opened for two new clubs to be embraced by the Bell's Divisions. After a tense vote, Elgin City and Peterhead were invited to step through from the Highland League. Their introduction provided a much-needed freshness to a lower division which, in recent years, had stagnated although the more distant location of their grounds was yet another financial hurdle for struggling clubs to overcome.

The annual battle just to stay afloat was becoming more difficult by the week for several cash-strapped clubs. Liquidators and the administrators were waiting in the wings, ready to take centre stage as the financial reality became too much for some clubs to shoulder. Yet, as with the start of every other season, 2000–1 brought with it hopes and dreams. This even made the quantum leap from club football to the international scene, where the fresh campaign to

For the game in this country to be vibrant, both halves of the Old Firm need to be offering a viable challenge for the honours

qualify for the World Cup finals in Japan and South Korea saw the disappointment of missing out on Euro 2000 filed under 'B' for 'blip'.

However, the road to the 2002 finals proved to be every bit as problematic for Craig Brown's side. And, after starting well, the national obsession with shooting ourselves in the foot crippled us once again, simultaneously bringing down the curtain on Scotland's World Cup campaign and the manager's career.

Truth be told, Craig Brown, like everyone else, had no idea what awaited fans of the Scottish game when the season moved into top gear. Certainly few could have predicted the season that was about to unfold, and even fewer could understand how the revolutionary split in the SPL programme would work. The intention was laudable enough. To facilitate 12 teams in the top division, a plan was required which would prevent clubs having to play 44 League games. After much deliberation it was agreed that the top and bottom six clubs would split after 33 League games had been played. Then came the difficult part. The fixture planners would have to try and decide in advance who would finish in which half of the table. By so doing they could avoid anyone having to play any other side away from home more than twice. Of course, there was never any hope of the predictions proving 100 per cent accurate – Ivano Bonetti's improving Dundee side saw to that. However, whilst Dundee may have upset the fixture compilers, they delighted thousands of fans across the country with their cavalier approach to both playing and signing players.

Argentinian World Cup star Claudio Caniggia joining up at Dens Park was the coup of the season. However, even this was not the big story of 2000–1. That is told in the chapters which follow. And what an amazing tale it is.

David Zitelli of Hibs gets past Livingston's Paul Deas as he helps his team through to meet Celtic in the Scottish Cup finals

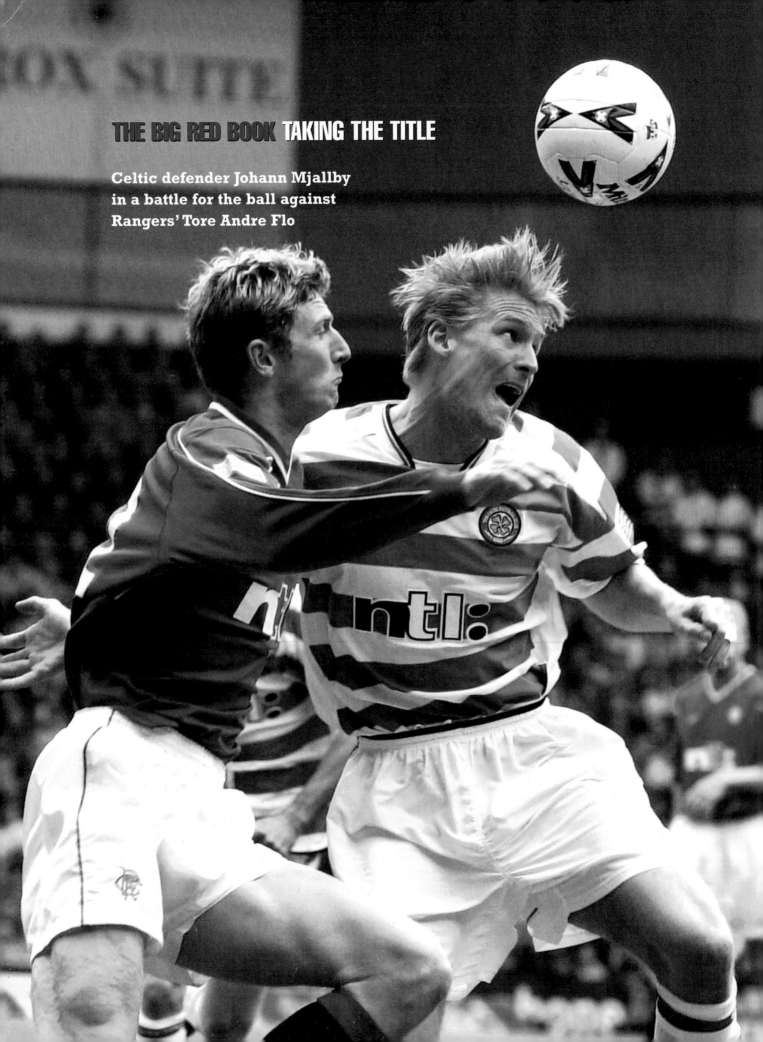

Celtic defender Johann Mjallby
in a battle for the ball against
Rangers' Tore Andre Flo

TAKING THE TITLE

It was party time at Ibrox once again on Saturday, 29 July 2000, and the invitation to come along and see the SPL championship flag unfurled was happily accepted by 52,000 Rangers fans. Sprinkled among them were a few hundred St Johnstone supporters, but the men from Perth knew this was going to start as Rangers' day and, almost certainly, would finish that way, too. Mind you, when defender Alan Kernaghan stole forward to acrobatically fire in the opening goal of the game, the men from Perth began to look like party poopers.

Ironically, it was one of Saints' former heroes, Billy Dodds, who ensured the result did not prove an embarrassment for the massed home support. He banged in a double, and Rangers were off and running in the League. Dodds had already got their European season off to a winning start, scoring two of Rangers' goals in the 4–1 home win over Lithuanian unknowns, Zalgiris Kaunas, in the first leg of their second-round Champions League qualifier. But Dodds was not the only man to be making headlines on the first day of the SPL season. Dundee's new player/boss, Ivano Bonetti, went from two jobs to none as he was sent off in his side's 2–0 win at Motherwell. Kilmarnock were the other first-day winners, Gary Holt's goal enough to take the points at Love Street as newly promoted St Mirren discovered that it was going to be a tough slog in the top flight. The other SPL new boys, Dunfermline, at least managed to make their point, holding Aberdeen to a goalless draw at East End Park.

All this was watched with great interest by Celtic fans, who had to wait another 24 hours before Martin O'Neill could send his side out for their first League game under his charge. That was at Tannadice, where Henrik Larsson wasted no time in getting back into scoring mode, putting Celtic one-up in the first half with a sweet curling shot from the edge of the United area. David McCracken stunned the visitors when he fired an equaliser past Jonathan Gould. But, as if scripted, O'Neill's first signing, £6 million-man Chris Sutton, stepped forward in the closing minutes to knock in the winner and get his and his manager's Celtic careers off to a winning start. Thrills and spills all the way to the end, unlike the fare produced at Tynecastle a few hours later as Hibs and Hearts shared the points, but no goals, in the first derby of the season.

AUGUST

Rangers had little time to reflect on their opening day success in what proved to be a busy opening week. They sold Jonatan Johansson to Charlton for £3.25m but refused to sell Neil McCann to Coventry, who had bid £4m for the winger. None of this distracted them from the business in hand, the second leg of their Champions League qualifier against Valgiris Kaunas in which they drew 0–0 to go through 4–1. And, by the second Saturday of the League season, they were back on the goal trail, knocking four past Kilmarnock at Rugby Park, another Dodds double helping the champions come back from 2–0 down, both Killie goals being scored by an in-form Andy McLaren.

The Rangers recovery was aided by the dismissal of Killie defender Kevin McGowne, and there were more red cards shown at Parkhead, where Celtic had to fight all the way to defeat Motherwell 1–0, thanks to a Stilian Petrov goal. Sutton discovered his robust style was not always going to be appreciated by Scottish referees as he was sent off by Alan Freeland after tangling with Greg Strong. Joining him in the sin bin was Jackie McNamara. But the ref wasn't finished there, with

Alex Smith took over the reins at Dundee United

'Well boss Billy Davies also seeing red and being banished to the stand.

Dundee continued their good start, even without suspended player/boss Bonetti, winning 3–0 at home to Dunfermline. But St Mirren's learning curve extended a little further as they lost 2–1 at Pittodrie.

Hearts collected their second point, this time with a 2–2 draw at McDiarmid Park, while Hibs began to show some of the form that would make them a major force over the course of the season with a comfortable 3–0 victory over Dundee United. It was a defeat too far for United boss Paul Sturrock, who resigned 24 hours later before picking up the threads of his career several weeks later at Plymouth.

Alex Smith and Maurice Malpas were in charge of the Tannadice side by the time they ran out to face Motherwell on Saturday, August 12, and no one had a grouse about that as United got their first point with a 1–1 draw. Dunfermline and St Johnstone also finished 1–1, but Hibs continued to catch the eye with a 5–1 hammering of Dundee after the Dens Park side's Billio and Caballero were sent off, sparking accusations of racism from Dundee.

The Old Firm were held back until Sunday as both had played midweek European ties, Rangers winning 3–0 away over Herfolge, while Celtic opened their UEFA Cup account with a 4–0 victory over Luxembourg side Jeunesse Esche. Back on SPL duty, Jorg Albertz hit a double as Rangers defeated St Mirren 3–1 at Love Street, while Celtic beat Kilmarnock 2–1 after Killie's Martin Baker had been sent off. Hearts made it three draws out of three when they were held 1–1 at Pittodrie.

The first midweek League game of the season shot Hibs, boosted by the signing of David Zitelli from Strasbourg, into the top spot in the table courtesy of their 1–0 win at Kilmarnock. Dunfermline won by the same margin at Motherwell. It was the Pars' first victory in the top flight, but it came against a side squabbling over a bonus structure.

The third weekend of the campaign was marked by goals, with Rangers – who had sold Paul Ritchie to Manchester City for £500,000 in that week – winning 4–1 at home to Dunfermline and Celtic emerging from Tynecastle with a 4–2 victory. But neither could remove Hibs from the top of the table after they won 2–0 at Aberdeen. At the other end there was relief for St Mirren, who notched up their first SPL win, 2–1 at home to Dundee, but Dundee United still struggled, losing 2–1 at Tannadice to St Johnstone, and Motherwell's problems increased after they lost a five-goal thriller at Kilmarnock.

It was the final weekend of August, and the SPL was about to explode! Rangers had just booked their place in the Champions League group stage with a 3–0 win over Herfolge, while Celtic got through to the UEFA Cup proper with an 11–0 aggregate win over Jeunesse Esche.

The perfect build-up to the first Old Firm game of the season, which had been eagerly awaited – not least by Martin O'Neill, who was about to experience its unique atmosphere for the first time. Little did he know it was to be one of the most memorable in the history of the fixture, bringing the biggest Celtic win since 1957 and providing the launch pad for the Parkhead club's championship challenge.

Sunday, 27 August, will be etched forever in the minds of all Hoops' fans as the day that Celtic thrashed Rangers 6–2. Sutton opened the scoring after only 52 seconds, and goals from Petrov and Paul Lambert saw them 3–0 up within 12 minutes. A second-half double from Larsson plus another from Sutton sealed an emphatic victory, with Rangers' only response a goal from Claudio Reyna and a Dodds' penalty. For Rangers' playmaker Barry Ferguson, the agony did not end there as he was sent off near the end of a dramatic 90 minutes.

O'Neill described the win as a 'fantastic' occasion. 'We got off to a great start, but there were plenty of uncomfortable moments. It could have been 3–2 after the first 17 or 18 minutes of the match, but you can't take anything away from the effort of the players. They were absolutely fantastic. Even at 4–1, I was thinking there's a long, long way to go. They got back to 4–2, and I think the only time I ever really felt comfortable was when Sutton put the sixth one in. But, at the end of it all – and I am not being patronising – Rangers are still the benchmark and are a top-class side. We couldn't have dreamed of a better start. We could play for another 100

Dundee player-manager Ivano Bonetti has put together one of the most entertaining teams in the country, not to mention introducing Claudio Caniggia to the SPL

Super Swede Henrik Larsson takes the acclaim of the crowd after scoring Celtic's fourth goal in the 6–2 defeat of Rangers at Parkhead

Only 12 minutes on the clock and Paul Lambert celebrates Celtic's third goal against Rangers at the first Old Firm encounter

A typically tough Old Firm battle, this time between Stilian Petrov and Rod Wallace

The expression on the face of goalkeeper Stefan Klos is one of disbelief at the end of the first Old Firm clash of the season

years and not get a start like that again. I'm delighted, and the players were brilliant. The performance was really, really immense. I would have settled for scoring in the last minute and winning the game 1–0.'

By contrast to the emotional and jubilant O'Neill, Advocaat promised to wield the axe, with new boy Fernando Ricksen – who was subbed in the first half – one of the targets.

'The back four were very poor,' Advocaat blasted. 'You can't afford to make mistakes like that at this level because you will get punished. That's just not good enough, and Ricksen was one of those players who was very poor. There is no doubt I'll be making changes because that kind of defending is just not acceptable. There is no doubt this was the worst game we have played since I have been here. We were very poor, and they looked like they would score with every attack.'

It was difficult to believe, but this was not the only game of the weekend. Aberdeen and Motherwell fought out a 1–1 draw, while Hearts, the treble chance specialist, did the same with Dundee at Dens. And 24 hours earlier, Hibs continued to sail along with a 2–0 win over St Mirren, Dunfermline kept Dundee United in bottom spot with a 1–0 win at East End Park, and Kilmarnock drew 1–1 at McDiarmid Park.

SEPTEMBER

Scotland's World Cup qualifier in Latvia provided a break in the SPL action, but Rangers responded to their hammering at Celtic Park by signing Ronald De Boer from Barcelona and attempting to capture John Hartson from Wimbledon, only for the move to collapse when the striker failed a medical.

Not to be outdone, Celtic signed Alan Thompson from Aston Villa, and Didier Agathe joined from Hibs while allowing Rafael Scheidt to join Corinthinans in Brazil on loan for a year. By the next weekend, the fuel protests were dominating the front pages of the newspapers, but Rangers got a major boost with the return of Michael Mols to the first team after ten months out. The Dutch striker helped secure a 1–1 draw at Dens Park.

Rangers boss Dick Advocaat feels the strain against Celtic

Action men: Rangers' Ronald de Boer and Celtic's Alan Thompson

But there was no stopping the Celtic rollercoaster as O'Neill – named Manager of the Month – saw his side knock Hibs off top spot with a 3–0 win over the men from the east. The joy was almost as tangible for Motherwell, who finally got their first League win of the season, a 1–0 victory at Love Street. Hearts also got off the mark, defeating Dunfermline 2–0.

With Celtic not playing until Monday after beating Helsinki 2–0 in the UEFA Cup on Thursday, Hibs returned to the top of the table on 16 September with a 2–0 win over Motherwell. Rangers, fresh from thumping Sturm Graz in their first Champions League group game, kept up the pressure thanks to Ronald De Boer's goal, which gave them all three points against Hearts. But Dundee United's nightmare continued as they were held to a goalless draw at home by St Mirren, only United's second point in seven games. Larsson gave

Dunfermline the Monday blues when his double powered Celtic back to the top with a 2–1 win at East End Park.

The midweek highlight was the Dundee derby, with United losing 3–0 at Dens, a defeat felt most acutely by Jason de Vos who was sent off for a wild tackle that virtually ended Dark Blues' striker Fabian Caballero's season. Down at Tynecastle, Hearts moved a little further up the table with a 2–0 victory over St Mirren, who were still struggling to last the pace, particularly in front of goal.

Michael Mols was back on the goal standard at Motherwell on Saturday, 23 September, his effort giving Rangers – fresh from another Champions League win, this time in Monaco – all three points, while Petrov was doing a similar job for Celtic against Dundee at Parkhead. It was Celtic's 12th straight win of the season.

Dundee United doubled their goals' tally for the

Ronald de Boer soaks up the applause after his goal against Hearts at Ibrox

OCTOBER

campaign but still crashed 5–3 to Aberdeen. Hibs dropped two points further behind Celtic after a 1–1 draw at Dunfermline, while Kilmarnock recorded a fine 2–0 win at Tynecastle and St Johnstone won the battle of the Saints at Love Street in a 1–0 win.

The final weekend of September saw St Mirren give debuts to new signings, one-time £1.3m-rated striker Graham Fenton and Dutchman Mikael Renfurm. They helped the Buddies defeat Dunfermline 2–1 at Love Street.

The following day, Celtic fans made the wrong sort of headlines when an assistant referee was struck by a coin while running the line in their match at Aberdeen. Bobby Petta was also in trouble after being sent off as the Dons took the first points of the season off Celtic, holding O'Neill's side to a 1–1 draw. It had been a difficult few days for Celtic, as they had only just got past Helsinki in their UEFA Cup tie in midweek after extra time.

Rangers were also on the rebound when they faced Dundee United at Ibrox, this time from a 3–2

Champions League defeat in Turkey against Galatasaray. But they bounced back in style by winning 3–0, helped by Marco Negri who started his first top team game for two and a half years.

Hibs finally got a return on their investment in David Zitelli when he got his first goal for the club in their 3–0 win at St Johnstone. Kilmarnock dropped two further points off the pace when they played out a 0–0 draw at Dundee. Hearts' veteran striker Gordon Durie notched up a double against Motherwell at Tynecastle as Hearts beat Motherwell – who had had Ange Oueifio sent off – 3–0.

The next weekend was blank for the SPL as the Scotland team took on San Marino in a World Cup qualifier before heading to Zagreb to face Croatia. But the action returned with a thump – literally! – on Saturday, 14 October, when there were unsavoury scenes at Tannadice following Dundee United's 4–0 defeat by Hearts. United's chairman and general manager, Jim McLean, was alleged to have assaulted BBC reporter John Barnes during a post-match interview live on TV. Police investigated but did not proceed with any charges. Nevertheless, McLean resigned from all positions at the club.

Back on the field, Hibs underlined that they were in for the long haul by beating Rangers 1–0 at Easter Road, with Zitelli scoring the only goal in a match that also saw Andrei Kanchelskis sent off. Across in Glasgow, goalkeeper Robert Douglas watched his new Celtic team-mates from the stand after completing his £1.2m move from Dundee. He saw Agathe named Man of the Match after he made his debut for the Hoops and helped dispose of St Mirren 2–0.

An even bigger name made his debut for Dundee. Argentinian World Cup star Claudio Caniggia appeared in a dark blue shirt for the first time as the Dens Park side won 2–0 at Aberdeen. Kilmarnock came from behind to beat Dunfermline 2–1 at Rugby Park, courtesy of a dubious penalty award, and Hearts hammered four past Dundee United at Tannadice. Motherwell also hit four as they got their second win of the season by beating St Johnstone 4–0 at Fir Park.

Claudio Caniggia has now changed his Dundee strip for a Rangers one

Hibs striker David Zitelli shows St Johnstone's Jim Weir a clean pair of heels during the 3–0 win for the Easter Road side

At this point the League was as follows.

PREMIER LEAGUE OCTOBER 2000

	P	W	D	L	F	A	Pt
CELTIC	10	9	1	0	24	8	28
HIBERNIAN	11	8	2	1	20	5	26
RANGERS	10	7	1	2	21	13	22
KILMARNOCK	11	6	2	3	14	11	20
HEARTS	11	4	4	3	17	11	16
DUNDEE	11	4	4	3	14	10	16
ABERDEEN	10	2	5	3	11	13	11
ST JOHNSTONE	10	2	5	3	9	15	11
DUNFERMLINE	11	2	3	6	8	17	9
MOTHERWELL	11	2	2	7	9	15	8
ST MIRREN	11	2	1	8	6	16	7
DUNDEE UNITED	11	0	2	9	6	25	2

In midweek, Joos Valgaeren got his name on the scoresheet for the first time as he opened the scoring for Celtic at McDiarmid Park. A more regular scorer, Larsson, made it 2–0 to secure the points. And the Parkhead side were still in unstoppable form by the weekend when a 2–1 home win over Dundee United kept them on top of the SPL table.

Joos Valgaeren was one of the major defensive platforms on which Celtic's success was built last season

Kilmarnock moved into third spot, their highest position of the season, with a 2–1 win over St Mirren, while Motherwell enjoyed a rare away victory, winning 2–1 at Dens Park.

Rangers, who had been held to a goalless draw by Galatasaray in midweek but remained top of the Champions League group, still trailed Celtic by 12 points in the SPL. And, after facing St Johnstone in Perth, the gap remained the same. Dick Advocaat accused his players of being bigheads and being more interested in their websites after they lost 2–1 to the Saints. Seldom seen so angry, the Rangers' manager left his stars in no doubt that they would have to buck up or log off.

Alex McLeish was a much happier manager, and little wonder – he had just watched his Hibs side crush Hearts 6–2 in the Edinburgh derby to emphasise their superiority in capital letters. Mixu Paatelainen was the star of the show, grabbing a hat-trick with some clinical finishing.

Motherwell's Northern Ireland international winger, Stuart Elliott, stole the headlines from Claudio Caniggia at Dens Park when he scored twice in a 2–1 win over the Dark Blues.

Alex McLeish – the Hibs boss has made them a real force again in Scotland

Motherwell's Stuart Elliott has forced himself into the Northern Ireland side

Kilmarnock manager Bobby Williams gives vent to his feelings at a training session

Kilmarnock leapfrogged Rangers in the Premier table with a 2–1 win over struggling St Mirren at Rugby Park. Andy McLaren and Alan Mahood were on target for Bobby Williamson's men, and Aberdeen and Dunfermline fought out a dour 0–0 draw at Pittodrie.

The final weekend in October saw Rangers under real pressure. They had crashed 2–0 away to Sturm Graz in the Champions League to put their qualification from the group in real doubt, but Advocaat hoped they could get back on a even keel when Kilmarnock came to Ibrox on League business. How wrong he was! His side were sunk without trace. Goals from Christophe Cocard, Andy McLaren and an own goal from Arthur Numan gave Bobby Williamson's side a well-deserved victory and Advocaat more food for thought as they trailed Celtic by 13 points.

Amid the worst spell to date of his time as manager of the club, Advocaat blasted, 'Rangers can still get there – I have faith in my players. There is nothing that cannot be sorted out. The squad

appears to have lost confidence and that is an element which I shall work upon immediately.

'I do not consider this to be a crisis, because we do have good players, many of whom are injured,' he added, 'but I am not using this as an excuse. I am responsible, as are the players on the pitch. I do accept we have problems, and they are quite serious at the moment. Yet, although the position is not good, we are still involved in all competitions.'

One of the men who added to Rangers' woes was former Ibrox hero Ian Durrant, and he backed Advocaat's view that they could fight their way out of their damaging slump.

'There are enough big boys in the Rangers' dressing room to sort it out,' he said, 'and it's down to them. It was a great day for us – to come to Ibrox and play like that is fantastic.'

It was also another good day for Hibs, who kept up the pressure on Celtic with a 1–0 victory at Tannadice. But there were few happy faces at Tynecastle after Hearts lost 3–0 to St Johnstone, sparking a protest from home fans after the game.

The following day, Celtic, buoyed by their draw in Bordeaux in midweek, stretched their lead over Rangers, but only by a single point. They shared the points in a thrilling six-goal game at Fir Park. St Mirren gave themselves some respite with their third League win of the season when they beat Aberdeen 2–0 at Love Street to move eight points clear of Dundee United at the bottom. Dunfermline also recorded a vital win, beating Dundee 1–0 at East End Park.

NOVEMBER

The first Saturday of the month brought some respite for troubled Rangers and fireworks from striker Kenny Miller. He stole the show with five goals in the 7–1 home win over shell-shocked St Mirren. How Dundee United could have used a sharp-shooter of his calibre. They continued to find it hard going, losing 2–1 at Motherwell.

Kenny Miller of Rangers is one of the brightest young strikers in the Scottish game

Twenty-four hours later a single Alan Thompson goal at Kilmarnock was enough to keep the Celtic winning machine rolling, but there was a down side to the day, with Paul Lambert suffering a stress fracture that would keep him out until January. Celtic knew they could ill afford to lose such an influential player, as Hibs – with Alex McLeish and Mixu Paatelainen named Manager and Player of the Month – refused to be shaken off their tails and had another good away day, winning 2–1 at Dundee.

With November only seven days old, the SPL suffered its second managerial casualty. Jim Jefferies left Hearts by mutual consent, while his assistant, Billy Brown, was sacked. Coach Peter Houston took over as interim manager as JJ and BB headed for the English Premiership with Bradford.

The mood was not much better back in Glasgow, where both Rangers and Celtic suffered major Euro blows. The Ibrox side crashed out of the Champions League after drawing at home to Monaco, while Celtic went out of the UEFA Cup after losing an extra-time goal to Bordeaux. That left both to concentrate fully on the championship race, and Celtic continued to set the pace with a resounding 4–1 home win over St Johnstone. Henrik Larsson's double brought to an end his mini-drought in front of goal.

Rangers found it harder going at Pittodrie, where they had to come from behind to defeat the Dons 2–1. The Pittodrie side had a mountain to climb after Derek Young was red-carded. The game would later become infamous for the first use of video evidence, Rangers' Fernando Ricksen being cited for a kick at Darren Young.

Twenty-four hours earlier, Hibs had missed the chance to go top when they could draw only 1–1 with Kilmarnock. There was a clear winner on Tayside, however, where Dundee underlined their supremacy in the city by dumping United 2–0.

Motherwell were another team to collect three points, with a rare 2–1 away win at Dunfermline. Peter Houston celebrated the same winning scoreline at Love Street, where Hearts were victorious in his first game in interim charge, and he wasted no time in announcing that he would be delighted to be considered for the post on a permanent basis. Sadly for him, Houston had a problem a week later when Celtic crushed his Hearts team 6–1 at Parkhead. It was an all-round good day for Martin O'Neill's leaders as Hibs

Fernando Ricksen has now settled into the Scottish game after a shaky start

suffered a shock 2–0 home defeat at the hands of Aberdeen and Rangers were held 0–0 at Dunfermline. There was no such shortage of goals at Dens Park, however, where a Caniggia double was the highlight of Dundee's 5–0 hammering of St Mirren. Fans who attended the match at McDiarmid Park between St Johnstone and Dundee United had to settle for a single goal, and that was enough to keep the points at home.

The next week saw TV game show *Who Wants To Be a Millionaire* pay out its first-ever £1m prize to contestant Judy Keppel, but Rangers' fans were more interested in their own new multi-million pound man – a Scottish signing record – and an amazing turnaround in the Old Firm's fortunes. Although they were not to know it at the time, Sunday, 26 November, was to be the highlight of Rangers' season, and new £12m signing from Chelsea, Tore Andre Flo, got his Ibrox career off to the best possible start when he scored in the 5–1 demolition of Celtic.

Barry Ferguson opened the scoring, but this was cancelled out just after the break by Larsson. Flo put Rangers back in front, and then Celtic suffered the hammer blow of Alan Thompson being sent off for his second booking for fouls on Ferguson. Ronald De Boer made it 3–1, and it was no surprise when Lorenzo Amoruso and Michael Mols completed the rout.

Flo was understandably delighted with his debut.

'The atmosphere was unbelievable,' he said. 'Everything people said about it was true. I have never faced a challenge like this match as a player and, after the excitement of signing a new contract and then this game, I am relieved. It has been an amazing week, with the christening of my daughter on Saturday.'

His manager, Advocaat, was entitled to be just as pleased and said, 'I am very happy, not just because of the result, but because of the commitment and the way we played. I have said all along you can replace one or two injured players, but not six or seven. When we have all our players available, we can beat anybody. The team showed what they can do today. The defence did well against two players of excellent quality in Sutton and Larsson. In the 6–2 game, Celtic scored two quick goals, and we could have done the same today – but we got the goals in the end.'

'We have to give Flo a little bit more time,' Advocaat added, 'but the good thing is he scored the goal at the right time.'

It was the first domestic defeat for O'Neill, and he admitted, 'Rangers deserved to beat us, but I don't think any manager likes to concede goals as cheaply as we did today. We defended poorly from corners, but Rangers were the better side. We didn't play well enough to cause any problems in the first half. Of course, Rangers were up for the game, but we can play much better. It's not the end of the world – or maybe it is. The run is over, let's get started again. It's going to be tight, but I believed that before the season started and, in fact, would have been delighted if we had made it tight. Rangers mean business and have showed that by spending £12m on a player. They won't give up lightly.'

Rangers' towering defender Lorenzo Amoruso in ecstatic mood after scoring Rangers' fourth goal in their 5–1 win over their Old Firm rivals

While Celtic were licking their wounds after suffering their first League defeat of the season, at Tannadice 24 hours earlier Dundee United had been celebrating their first League win of the campaign. A last-minute penalty converted by Charlie Miller secured a 3–2 win over Dunfermline.

St Mirren also scored in the final minute to hold Hibs to a 1–1 draw while Keigan Parker confirmed his potential with both goals in St Johnstone's win at Kilmarnock. Hearts were also winners, romping to a 3–1 victory against a Dundee side proving to be the real enigma of the SPL.

The month closed with midweek action and an injury that will live in the memory of all who saw it. Dundee United's Jamie Fullarton, still trying to

Rangers paid a record £12 million for striker Tore Andre Flo – who scores on his Old Firm debut

It's a pensive Martin O'Neill during Celtic's Old Firm defeat

establish himself after arriving from Crystal Palace, was the victim during the 1–0 defeat by Kilmarnock at Tannadice on Tuesday, 28 November. He went in for a challenge with Killie's James Fowler, and it was immediately clear he was in serious trouble.

Fortunately, the United physio and club doctor recognised his plight and raced to his side. The doctor managed to manipulate his dislocated ankle back into position, an action that it was later revealed saved the player's foot as the blood supply had been stopped. After the horrific scene, the result was almost incidental, but it did propel Killie into the third spot, ahead of Rangers. By comparison, the goalless draw fought out between St Johnstone and Aberdeen was a tame affair.

Twenty-four hours later there was another goalless draw, but this one was far more significant. Celtic, still smarting from their whipping at Ibrox, passed this test of character at Easter Road, much to Hibs' disappointment as they had hoped to eat into their seven-point lead.

The match between Motherwell and St Mirren also looked to be ending in stalemate until a late double from the home side snatched the points, while Dunfermline also emerged as winners, defeating Hearts by a single goal.

DECEMBER

That game was to be Houston's last in charge of the Tynecastle side, as former skipper Craig Levein was appointed head coach on the opening day of December. His first game in charge, two days later, was a cracker, Rangers emerging as 1–0 winners despite having Claudio Reyna and Arthur Numan sent off. Both errant players were later revealed to have received a further yellow card from referee Stuart Dougal for not leaving the field quickly enough when sent off, a disciplinary problem that only added to Advocaat's difficulties as injuries were still depriving him of other key personnel. But at least they had won their UEFA Cup third-round match against Kaiserslautern in midweek, so things were finally starting to look up for the Ibrox club. They still trailed in fourth place, however, as Hibs kept up the pressure on Celtic with a 3–1 win at Motherwell.

Martin O'Neill's side had got back on the winning trail the day before, coming from behind to win 3–1 against Dunfermline at Parkhead. Kilmarnock also continued to enjoy a purple patch, winning 2–1 at Pittodrie, while St Johnstone scored a late equaliser to finish 1–1 at Dens Park.

Rangers' Arthur Numan beats Hearts' Colin Cameron to the ball

Craig Levein returns to Tynecastle as their new manager midway through the season

St Johnstone's Keigan Parker shields the ball from Dundee's Marco de Marchi

Strugglers St Mirren and Dundee United had to wait until Tuesday before they could lock horns at Love Street. The 1–1 draw was more appreciated by the Saints, who had had Tom Brown sent off.

Rangers' revival proved short-lived as they crashed out of the UEFA Cup in Kaiserslautern, but they took some solace from their 2–0 home win over Motherwell. This fired them ahead of Kilmarnock in the table after Bobby Williamson's side went down 3–0 to Hearts at Rugby Park. Hibs defeated Dunfermline by the same scoreline, while St Johnstone won the latest battle of the Saints at McDiarmid Park 2–0 as the Paisley side's lack of firepower continued to cost them dear.

Unusually, Celtic also found it tough to get goals the following day as, once more, Dundee succeeded in keeping Larsson and Sutton quiet. Tom Boyd did manage to get on the scoresheet at Dens Park, but for the wrong side, his own goal equalising Stilian Petrov's opener. And it took Didier Agathe's last-minute close-in effort – his first goal for Celtic – to take the points in a match that left debutant Neil Lennon breathless.

He had arrived in a £6m move from Leicester three days earlier and admitted, 'This has been a big, big week for me, and I'm more mentally than physically tired. I have not really trained properly in the past week, so I am just really pleased with the way things have gone. We scored the goal at the best possible time and probably deserved it with the chances we had.

'Dundee is a hard place to obtain three points,' Lennon added prophetically, 'but this is what wins championships.'

Eoin Jess was a notable absentee from the Aberdeen side that travelled to Ibrox the following Wednesday after the Scotland player had criticised his club's ambition. He must have felt like eating his words as Arild Stavrum opened the scoring, but then the roof fell in on the Dons as goals from Mols, Dodds and Albertz wrapped up the win.

The Pittodrie side had to return to Glasgow three days later, this time to face Celtic – and this time they were hit for six. Star of the show was Hoops' new Bhoy, Ramon Vega, O'Neill's seventh and final signing of the season. The Swiss defender, who had been frozen out at Spurs, was an instant hit, scoring two goals in the 6–0 rout. Not to be outshone, Larsson rattled in a hat-trick and sub Jamie Smith made it six.

Kilmarnock also thought they were cruising to victory at home to Dundee as they raced to a 2–0 lead. But the visitors fought back to win a five-goal thriller. Hibs did manage to hold on to their 2–0 lead against St Johnstone, and Dunfermline managed to win by the same scoreline against St Mirren.

Yet another 2–0 scoreline was recorded in favour of home side Motherwell in their game against Hearts, with boss Billy Davies singing the praises of goalkeeper Andy Goram. The Fir Park chief said, 'We had Andy to thank for some outstanding saves.'

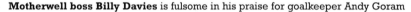

Motherwell boss Billy Davies is fulsome in his praise for goalkeeper Andy Goram

Aberdeen's
Thomas Solberg
and Kevin McNaughton
get the ball away from
Rangers' Ronald de Boer

The big Sunday game was at Tannadice, where an Amoruso blunder let United's new signing Derek Lilley in to equalise against Rangers, prompting more calls for the big Italian to be replaced.

Pop superstar Madonna was the main focus of the news on the weekend before Christmas as she was married to Guy Ritchie at Skibo Castle. On the back pages, however, there was an early present for Rangers in the shape of three vital points against Hibs. Ronald de Boer got the only goal of the game at Ibrox, which saw Jorg Albertz and John O'Neil sent off.

Along the M8 at Love Street, Celtic were motoring to a 2–0 win over St Mirren to stretch their lead at the top of the table. Motherwell were also away winners, emerging as 3–2 victors over St Johnstone, despite having Derek Adams sent off.

Boxing Day brought a belated reason to celebrate for Kilmarnock striker Paul Wright. He scored his first-ever senior hat-trick in the 3–1 win at Love Street. Henrik Larsson also reached a milestone when he grabbed his 60th SPL goal in Celtic's 4–0 win at Tannadice.

But it was a season of mixed emotions for Rangers' Fernando Ricksen. He was alleged to have failed a breath test over Christmas but still managed to score his first goal for Rangers in their 3–0 home win over St Johnstone. Dunfermline sent their fans home happy after winning 3–2 against Aberdeen, while Dundee supporters who made the trip to Motherwell were pleased they did as they saw their side win 3–0. In the third Edinburgh derby of the season, it was honours even as the match at Tynecastle finished 1–1.

The year went out with a bang for Dundee United keeper Alan Combe, who was reported by the referee for aiming a head-butt gesture at a linesman as he left the field following Hibs' 1–0 win at Easter Road. Combe had been unhappy at the awarding of a 97th-minute penalty, converted by Russell Latapy, but he denied making the gesture and was later found not guilty. The only other SPL game to survive the severe weather saw Hearts draw 2–2 with St Johnstone in Perth.

Fernando Ricksen scores his first goal for Rangers against St Johnstone

JANUARY

The New Year began as the old one had finished – with Celtic running riot! This time Kilmarnock were on the receiving end of four goals from Larsson and a double by Sutton. The four-timer brought the Swede's goal tally in a Celtic strip to 101, a feat that led Sutton to describe the Swede as 'priceless'.

In the final round of games before the winter break, Rangers were also happy to sign off with a victory. Flo got two of their goals in the 3–1 win at Love Street, a match that could have been Amoruso's last game in a Rangers strip as he then jetted off to have talks with West Ham. Hibs were also in winning form, defeating Dundee 3–0, while Dundee United got only their second three points of the campaign, winning 2–0 against Motherwell. Aberdeen, too, grabbed a much needed win, defeating Hearts by the only goal at Pittodrie, while St Johnstone and Dunfermline finished goalless. Saints' problems were not confined to the field, however. The Perth club was rocked by reports of alleged drug abuse by two of their players, George O'Boyle and Kevin Thomas, at a team night out. Both players were immediately sacked, but it took months of appeals to the SPL and the SFA before their contracts were finally ended.

Tore Andre Flo nets a double against St Mirren

At this point the placings were as follows:

PREMIER LEAGUE JANUARY 2001

	P	W	D	L	F	A	Pt
CELTIC	24	20	3	1	66	21	63
HIBERNIAN	25	16	6	3	44	15	54
RANGERS	23	16	3	4	50	24	51
KILMARNOCK	24	12	3	9	30	32	39
HEARTS	25	9	6	10	37	37	33
DUNDEE	23	8	6	9	34	28	30
DUNFERMLINE	24	8	6	10	22	30	30
ST JOHNSTONE	25	7	9	9	25	35	30
MOTHERWELL	24	8	4	12	30	38	28
ABERDEEN	23	4	9	10	24	39	21
ST MIRREN	24	3	3	18	15	48	12
DUNDEE UNITED	24	2	4	18	16	46	10

The St Johnstone story dominated throughout the winter shutdown, which saw Rangers and Celtic head to the warmer climes of Florida while Europe provided training facilities for the majority of the other SPL clubs. Not to be deprived of their football for too long, however, 50,000 auld Old Firm fans turned up at Ibrox to watch former heroes go head-to-head in aid of charity, a game won 4–1 by an Ally McCoist-inspired Rangers side.

By the end of the month it was action for real again as the third round of the Scottish Cup threw up no real upsets for the big boys, allowing them to concentrate once more on the championship. Hibs were first back into action, drawing 1–1 at Kilmarnock on Tuesday, 30 January, with both goals coming from defenders, Killie's Gary Hay and the visitors' Ulrik Laursen.

At least the fans at Rugby Park saw some goals. At McDiarmid Park the following night, the crowd who had packed in hoping to watch St Johnstone face Celtic could see nothing as Scottish football's first pay-per-view experiment descended into farce amid the descending mist. The cancellation allowed Rangers to close the gap on Celtic to nine points as Tugay scored the only goal in their win over Aberdeen at Ibrox.

The restart had also given Dundee United fresh hope, and they celebrated with a 3–2 win over Dundee at Dens Park. This eased United's relegation fears just a little, but St Mirren continued to find the going tough, especially in front of goal, and went down 1–0 at Tynecastle while Motherwell and Dunfermline were happy to settle for a goal and a point apiece at Fir Park.

Dundee striker Juan Sara and St Mirren defender Scott Walker do battle at Love Street

FEBRUARY

By the first Saturday of February, Celtic's lead in the table had been cut to just six points as Rangers continued to try to exert a little pressure. Their 2–0 home win over Dunfermline carried them back into second place in the table, helped by the postponement of Hibs' match at Pittodrie because of bad weather.

But while things were frozen off in the north, they were heating up at the south of the table where St Mirren got off the bottom spot, courtesy of a 2–1 home win over Dundee. Dundee United found themselves back in the relegation berth after being held 1–1 at home by St Johnstone. Kilmarnock were still looking for their first League win of 2001 after losing 2–1 at home to Motherwell.

The following day, any question about Celtic having the bottle to ignore the new challenge being thrown down by Rangers was quickly answered as Larsson hit a hat-trick to give them a 3–0 win and three points at a snowy Tynecastle. The lead was back to nine points, and Celtic were back in top gear. They had also managed to get the disruptive influence of Eyal Berkovic out of the camp as he joined Blackburn on loan until the end of the season, while at the same time welcoming Paul Lambert back after his stress fracture. But there was some bad news for O'Neill as the influential Joos Valgaeren went over on an ankle at Tynecastle. As the crack rang out around the ground, he appeared to have suffered a fracture that would keep him out for the remainder of the campaign. Fortunately for all concerned, the big Belgian was later confirmed to have sustained only a twist that would keep him out only for a couple of games.

What a couple of games they turned out to be as Celtic went into a double-header with Rangers. Their first clash was in the CIS League Cup semi-final at Hampden, which ended with Celtic winning the goal count 3–1 but losing the red-card count 2–1 as ref Willie Young sent off Reyna, Mols and Moravcik amid ugly scenes near the end of the tousy match. This added unwanted fuel to an already volatile third League meeting between the teams at Parkhead on Sunday, 11 February. The match was being billed as Rangers' last chance to stop Celtic romping away with the title, but for most neutrals it was viewed as another potentially explosive meeting of Glasgow's two tribes, with the eyes of the world upon them.

Fortunately, the game was remembered for what happened in terms of football and little else. Expertly handled by referee Hugh Dallas, the game ended 1–0, with Alan Thompson's close-in goal after a quarter of an hour all that separated the sides after 90 uneventful

Rangers' last chance to stop Celtic, or another potentially explosive meeting of Glasgow's two tribes?

minutes. Even the ubiquitous sending-off was low key, Fernando Ricksen getting his marching orders before the break for a second bookable offence.

So Celtic eased 12 points clear of Rangers with 12 games to go, but no one on either side of the great divide was prepared to concede it was all over. Celtic boss O'Neill admitted he planned to have a good night out after his side had beaten Rangers twice within four days but still preferred to analyse what had transpired rather than gloat.

'I thought we played brilliantly during the first half,' he said, 'but somehow we couldn't manage to kill the game, although we continued to make chances after Alan had scored the opening goal. Rangers got a bit of rhythm about their play in the second half, despite the fact they had been reduced to ten men by then, and they caused us a few problems.'

Clearly, however, his first season competing against their arch-Nemesis from across the city had gone better than he had dared dream.

'Our 6–2 win was very early on in my time at this club,' O'Neill reflected, 'and maybe it didn't strike home to Rangers. Perhaps they thought they had suffered a bad day at the office. We lost out heavily to them at Ibrox, and then won last Wednesday. This time, however, the two teams knew precisely what was at stake. We knew the importance of the game, and I'm just happy we have won it. Obviously, the players are very pleased, but I can assure you there is no sense of triumphalism within the dressing room.'

'At half-time,' he continued, 'when we were a goal ahead, we never gave a thought to the fact that we would be playing against ten men in the second half. We were fully aware that Rangers had to push forward and that they did. We coped, and we might well have scored a second goal when Alan Thompson sent his shot over the crossbar. It was a bit nervy because we couldn't manage to kill them off, but at the end of the day, we took the points.'

Rangers' manager Advocaat conceded that his side now faced a monumental task to peg back Celtic but refused to throw in the towel completely.

'We have to be realistic,' he said. 'It will now be very, very difficult to catch Celtic, but as long as it is still possible we have to believe in it. In football, everything is possible.

Rangers' goalkeeper Stefan Klos was one of the club's most consistent performers last year

'It was very important,' he added, 'that we scored the first goal. Instead, Celtic did, and they deserved to be 1–0 ahead at half-time. I think the way we played in the second half, we have to give the team credit. I think we played much better than in the first half and had some chances to score a goal. I'm not pleased with the first half, but they worked hard with ten men.'

Not that Advocaat was complaining about having yet another man sent off. He was more disappointed that his pre-match warnings had been ignored by fellow Dutchman Ricksen, who had been walking a tightrope after collecting his first booking after only 11 minutes.

'I said to them, the first tackle will be yellow or red, normally yellow,' Advocaat explained. 'Unfortunately, it was on our side.' But he praised the performance of the match officials and claimed, 'I think Hugh Dallas was excellent.'

The defeat kept Rangers in third place in the table as Hibs had climbed above them again the day before with a 4–2 win over St Mirren at Easter Road. With Celtic moving away from the chasing pack, that second spot in the table was becoming more and more significant as it brought with it a ticket to the qualifying rounds of the Champions League.

Kilmarnock also had their eyes on a European spot, and their 2–1 win over St Johnstone at Perth got them back on track for fourth spot and a UEFA Cup berth. The split was also looming large, and Dunfermline looked to be in good shape to defy the odds and make it into the top six. Their 3–1 home win over Dundee United brought another welcome three points.

Dundee's home clash against Hearts was postponed, and Aberdeen were just pleased to be keeping out of the relegation zone, a 1–0 win at Motherwell sending them back up the road happy.

The intervening Scottish Cup fourth round kept the SPL on hold until Wednesday, 21 February, but when it returned it did so with a thump. Motherwell's Scott Leitch was the man on the end of it as he limped out of the game at Parkhead following a challenge by Celtic striker Chris Sutton that 'Well boss Billy Davies later described as over

The task facing Hibs was daunting, but Libbra's equaliser against Celtic kept them in the hunt for the second Champions League spot

the top. Celtic boss O'Neill chose to ignore the accusations, preferring instead to concentrate on the wonderful free-kick by sub Lubo Moravcik, which was all that separated the teams at the end of a tricky match. O'Neill was later to include this victory among the most important of the season as the winning line moved ever closer.

Dunfermline continued to hold their place in the top half of the table with a 1–0 win at Dundee, while St Mirren's plight became ever more acute with a 3–0 hammering at Pittodrie.

The Buddies found themselves back in bottom spot by the last Saturday of February as they lost 1–0 at home to Motherwell. Dundee United clambered over them after taking a point in a poor goalless draw at Kilmarnock. Hearts proved to be the big hitters of the day, thumping seven past Dunfermline, who could only breach the Tynecastle defences once in reply. Aberdeen's home clash with St Johnstone fell victim to the weather, but Rangers got all three points at Dens Park when Bert Konterman's effort was enough to separate the teams. That win kept them right in touch with Hibs, who had to go to Celtic Park for the Sunday live TV game.

The task facing them was daunting as Celtic had not conceded a single point at home all season. But that was all to end, thanks to the loan signing from Toulouse of Marc Libbra. The sub took advantage of some slack defensive play to slot the ball under Rab Douglas and equalise Johan Mjallby's goal for Celtic. The result kept Hibs right in the hunt for the second Champions League spot, but Alex McLeish was already playing down their chances of beating Rangers to the runner-up's slot.

'I believe Rangers are the stronger side,' he said, 'and that, come the end of the season, they will prove that. The Old Firm still have this aura about them where they just go out and beat teams.'

For his counterpart, O'Neill, there were other issues to address, not least the offer of a place on the Celtic board.

'I know nothing about the suggestion,' he insisted. 'I can only say it is hard enough trying to manage this club without then going on the board and getting myself sacked.'

Bert Konterman blasts home for Rangers during their 3–1 win over Dundee at Dens Park

MARCH

March opened with good news and bad news for Rangers as Giovanni van Bronckhorst made his long-awaited comeback from injury – only to limp off after 23 minutes of the 2–0 home win over Hearts, who had Colin Cameron sent off. At least things were looking up for Dundee United, who had their best win of the season, a 4–0 thumping of relegation rivals St Mirren at Tannadice. Dundee also got three points after their 3–2 win over St Johnstone at Perth, but Killie and Aberdeen had to settle for one apiece after their goalless draw at Rugby Park.

The following day proved to be a super Sunday for Neil Lennon, who scored his first goal for Celtic in their 3–0 win at Dunfermline. This took the Hoops 13 points clear at the top of the table as a result of Hibs being held to a 1–1 draw by Motherwell at Easter Road. But it was not all good news for Celtic

as Chris Sutton damaged shoulder ligaments at East End Park, an injury that would keep him out until the League Cup final at the end of the month.

Once again the Scottish Cup halted the progress of the SPL and effectively ended Rangers' season as they crashed out to Dundee United at Tannadice. Dick Advocaat moved quickly to try to improve matters by signing Marcus Gayle from Wimbledon and taking Fabrice Fernandes on loan from Fulham.

Hibs were first to get back into League action, buoyed by booking their place in the quarter-finals of the Cup. But they were soon sunk again as Tuesday the 13th proved unlucky when they lost 1–0 at Pittodrie.

The bad breaks were even more acutely felt by Celtic the following night when they lost Stilian Petrov with a leg fracture during the 2–1 win over St Johnstone in Perth. The young Bulgarian went in for a tackle with Saints' Jim Weir, and it was immediately clear he was in big trouble. Goals from

Claudio Caniggia celebrates after scoring for Dundee against Rangers at Ibrox

Larsson and Tommy Johnson overcame Stuart McCluskey's effort for the home side and put Celtic 16 points clear of Rangers, who had lost 2–0 at home to Dundee, Claudio Caniggia and Steven Milne getting on the scoresheet. Craig Moore was sent off, the 12th red card picked up by a Rangers' player that season. Meanwhile, over at Tynecastle, Hearts were back in the hunt for a UEFA Cup place after defeating Kilmarnock 3–0.

Fabrice Fernandes became an instant hit with the Rangers' fans when he scored on his debut for the club at Motherwell on Saturday, 17 March. 'Well's Don Goodman also got on the scoresheet in his final game for the club before moving to Walsall, but Bob Malcolm was on hand to score the winner in the dying minutes, knocking the ball past Andy Goram who, within a few days, would be on his way to Manchester United.

Hibs' run of poor results continued with a 2–1 defeat at Dunfermline, but St Mirren got back into winning form with a crucial 1–0 victory at home against St Johnstone. Dundee and Hearts failed to find the net at Dens, but Dundee United and Aberdeen managed to score a goal apiece at Tannadice. Celtic and Kilmarnock were excused SPL duties as they had the little matter of the CIS League Cup Final to attend on Sunday, 18 March. Once again, there was no holding Larsson as he hit a hat-trick, aided by Sutton, until the Englishman was red-carded.

The nation lost one of its favourite sporting sons the next day as rugby legend Gordon Brown passed away after a long battle against cancer. He was 53.

The World Cup qualifiers against Belgium and San Marino were next to keep the SPL sides from making progress in the championship, and that weekend the JVC electronics plant in East Kilbride announced a novel plan to combat absenteeism after Old Firm games. The company said it had plans to bring in American-style 'duvet days' as staff were often hungover after watching televised Old Firm clashes on Sundays.

Aberdeen and St Johnstone were next in action, managing to squeeze in a game on Tuesday, 27 March, which ended 3–3. The programme picked

Hearts' Finnish goalkeeper Antti Niemi has turned in some outstanding performances for the Tynescastle club

APRIL

The following day, Rangers crashed at home once again, this time Dundee United emerging with three valuable points courtesy of their 2–0 win after Steven Thompson and Derek Lilley had exposed Rangers' defensive frailty. Hibs also suffered a 2–0 reverse, this time at McDiarmid Park, to open the door to an early championship finish for Celtic if they could win their final three games before the split. They got the first of them out of the way at Pittodrie that night, when Didier Agathe's goal was enough to separate the teams.

So the midweek game against Dundee at Parkhead on 4 April took on added significance for everyone connected with Celtic. Tommy Johnson, in for the suspended and injured Sutton, got the home side off to the best possible start, but the ever-dangerous Juan Sara equalised to set Celtic back on their heels. This brought the instruction from the dug-out for Johan Mjallby to take his massive frame forward in search of the winner. And the tactic paid

Celtic's Johann Mjallby battles against St Mirren's Stephen McPhee

up again in full on the final weekend of the month, and once more it was the split that was capturing the headlines. With one weekend to go until it happened, there were plenty of anxious faces around the mid-table clubs, and no one at Dunfermline was satisfied with the 1–1 draw they managed at Love Street. Dundee also drew, 2–2 with Kilmarnock, who had Craig Dargo sent off, to keep their hopes of a top-six place alive, and Hearts were delighted to win 3–0 at home against a Motherwell side now minus several regulars as the club continued to cut its wage bill.

off as the big Swede was on hand to knock the ball home from close range to put Celtic within touching distance of the title.

And so it was that on 7 April, Grand National day, St Mirren travelled to Parkhead, hoping to keep the champagne on ice. Tom Hendrie's side had an agenda of their own as they were still battling manfully to avoid relegation. But nothing was going to spoil Celtic's party, and it was Tommy Johnson who grabbed the all-important goal in the first half to secure the victory and the championship. The cocky Geordie would be the first to admit it was not the sweetest strike of his career. In fact, he let the ball slip under his foot before retrieving the situation by firing a shot under Ludovic Roy. Jamie McGowan almost managed to clear the effort off the line but succeeded only in knocking the ball into the roof of the net. Cue the laps of honour.

When O'Neill had caught his breath again, he paid tribute to the players who had turned around a 21-point advantage enjoyed by Rangers the previous season. But he wasted no time in setting them their next target.

'We have got to concentrate on the treble now,' O'Neill said. He admitted that, even as a former winner of the European Cup as a player, this day had been something exceptional.

'It is sensational to win it, and to win it at Celtic Park is everything, and more, than you dream of,' he said. 'The occasion was everything I wanted. It's as good a day as I've had in football, and I was lucky enough to have some decent days as a player. The fans were phenomenal, they really were. I'm finding it hard to describe. I think there was an apprehension during the game, maybe because we got ourselves in a good position and didn't want

Bhoy, what a party as the Celtic players hoop it up after sealing the title

to let it go. Maybe it was also that we've only won one championship in 12 years, and there was a bit of anxiety creeping in because we couldn't get the second goal. I knew today that if we couldn't win we still had plenty of opportunities to win the League, but I wanted it today. If we had scored a second I would maybe have been able to enjoy it more, but the final whistle was as pleasing a moment as I could imagine.'

'We have won 28 of the 33 matches that we have played,' he added, 'and I can't praise the players any higher. It is special to win the championship. As my old mentor, Brian Clough, used to say, the team that wins the championship is usually the best of the season.'

That was a sentiment echoed by Larsson, but he recognised a good team is only a winning team if managed properly.

'We didn't play well last season, that's a fact,' said the Swede, 'but you need someone to guide you and pull everything together and Martin has done that.'

There was also reason to celebrate for Dundee, who snatched a top-six place on the final day with a 2–0 victory at Aberdeen. But for every winner there must be a loser, and in this case it was Dunfermline, who slipped into the bottom half of the table after losing 2–1 at Kilmarnock, while Dundee United grabbed another crucial point in their 1–1 draw with Hearts.

The following day, Rangers managed to remain

Feeling just champion, Martin O'Neill takes a bow in front of ecstatic Celtic fans

Overjoyed Celtic fans savour the moment after watching their side wrap up the championship

six points clear of Hibs in second place when they emerged from Easter Road with a 0–0 draw. Motherwell managed to defeat St Johnstone 1–0, but for both clubs the season was effectively over.

Two days later the final loose end before the split was tidied up at Rugby Park when Rangers defeated Kilmarnock 2–1 thanks to a double by Flo. Garry Hay had given Killie some hope with a goal, but Ally McCoist saw his penalty saved by Stefan Klos to deny the home side a point.

THE PLACINGS

	P	W	D	L	F	A	Pt
CELTIC	33	28	4	1	81	24	88
RANGERS	32	21	4	7	58	30	67
HIBERNIAN	33	17	10	6	52	25	61
KILMARNOCK	32	14	7	11	38	42	49
HEARTS	33	13	8	12	52	44	47
DUNDEE	33	11	8	14	47	41	41
DUNFERMLINE	33	11	8	14	32	48	41
MOTHERWELL	33	11	6	16	37	48	39
ABERDEEN	33	8	12	13	37	48	36
ST JOHNSTONE	33	8	11	14	35	48	35
DUNDEE UNITED	33	5	8	20	30	58	23
ST MIRREN	33	5	4	24	21	64	19

The Scottish Cup semi-finals were all that fans had to keep them entertained while the SPL drew up their post-split programme of matches. But Rangers' fans already had plenty to think about as the television news bulletins and newspapers reported on the death of Ibrox legend Jim Baxter, who was aged 61 when he succumbed to cancer.

The present Rangers heroes got back into the winning groove with a 3–0 win at Dundee on 21 April. It took Advocaat's men even further away from Hibs, who were possibly already looking ahead to meeting Celtic in the Scottish Cup final after their 3–0 semi-final victory over Livingston. Whatever the reason, Alex McLeish's men appeared to have taken their eye off the ball as they could only draw 1–1 with Kilmarnock at Easter Road.

In the bottom half of the table, Aberdeen defeated Dunfermline 1–0 while St Johnstone enjoyed an identical victory at Motherwell. This left the stage clear for Celtic to be presented with the SPL trophy 24 hours later. There had been complaints that the presentation had not taken place following the victory over St Mirren two weeks earlier, but no one raised a dissenting voice when Tom Boyd stepped forward to receive the trophy following the 1–0 win over Hearts, a victory

Thumbs up from Alex McLeish and Andy Watson as Hibs make a good play

Dundee United's David Hannah beats St Mirren's Ricky Gillies in the battle to avoid relegation

St Mirren's Ricky Gillies knocks in a double against Dundee United

Battle of the little guys – Rod Wallace in a tussle with Lubo Moravcik

made possible by Moravcik's goal. O'Neill had insisted his players didn't allow the gloss to be taken off the occasion by losing the match, and again he took the opportunity to commend their professionalism. No one epitomised this better than Paul Lambert.

'We deserve this success,' he said. 'As you saw tonight, there's a work ethic about the team, which pays dividends. The facts speak for themselves. We've only lost one game all season. But this club needs success. Our fans demand it all the time.'

It was survival that occupied the minds of St Mirren and Dundee United two days later when

they clashed in a relegation dogfight at Love Street. Thompson gave the visitors the lead, but local hero Ricky Gillies hit back with a double to give the Buddies hope in the closing four games. And their bid to beat the drop took another important step forward the following weekend, when Saints won 2–1 at Dunfermline. Dundee United refused to throw in the towel, however, and gained a much needed three points themselves with a 1–0 home win over Motherwell as Aberdeen won 3–0 just down the road at Perth. But the result that really caught the eye that weekend came 24 hours later when Celtic crushed Rangers 3–0 at Ibrox. Henrik Larsson

Jackie McNamara nets twice against Hibs in the League

chose this moment to knock in his 50th goal of an astonishing season while Lubo Moravcik grabbed the other two, the second of which was set up by 17-year-old debutant Shaun Maloney.

Larsson was delighted to reach this milestone, but he reserved most of his praise for team-mate Moravcik. The Swede, who later that evening collected the PFA's Player of the Year award, said, 'It's not often you get the chance to play with someone as good as Lubo. His goals were tremendous, and, for me, the second was one of the best I have ever seen. In the first half we didn't create too many chances. But then Lubo did some

absolutely brilliant things, and that's why I love to play with him.'

'I am very happy with my record,' Larsson continued. 'It is not every season you get 50, and to do it at Ibrox feels good. There wasn't really any pressure on us because we had won the League already, and you can't go to Ibrox under better circumstances.' It was Celtic's fourth win of the season against Rangers and gave them revenge for the 5–1 drubbing they had suffered on their previous visit to Ibrox.

Away from the limelight, Hibs confirmed their place in the UEFA Cup with a 2–0 win at Dens Park.

MAY

By the first weekend in May, the Scottish Cup final was already dominating most thoughts as there was little business to be completed in the SPL. And Sunday, 6 May, threw up a dress-rehearsal for the Hampden finale when Celtic travelled to face Hibs at a sunny Easter Road.

O'Neill's men emerged as easy 5–2 winners, with the main talking point being the return to first-team action of Alan Stubbs following his successful battle against a recurrence of cancer. The big defender came on as a sub at half-time and announced his arrival with a goal. Jackie McNamara staked his claim for a Cup final place by scoring the first two, while Moravcik and Larsson got one apiece, the Swede's goal equalling Brian McClair's record of 35 Premier goals in a season, before Libbra restored some of Hibs' pride with a late double.

The day before, Rangers had visited the capital and trounced Hearts 4–1, but at a cost, as they had had Barry Ferguson sent off. He was soon joined in the tunnel by former Ibrox defender Steven Pressley, who was also red-carded.

Ricky Gillies was another man to see red as St Mirren lost an early lead and finished 2–2 at McDiarmid Park, a result made all the more painful when news reached them that Dundee United had beaten Dunfermline 1–0. Aberdeen continued to make a good finish to the season with a 2–0 win at Motherwell, while Killie lost 2–1 at Dens Park.

A place in the history books soon awaited Dundee, however, as they became the first side in over a year to win at Celtic Park in domestic competition. Fabian Caballero was the man who unpicked the Celtic defence with a double, all the more commendable considering Dundee had played with ten men for an hour after central defender Zura Khizanishvili was sent off. The defeat prevented Celtic from reaching the 100-point mark for the season, but the day did not end without

Hearts Antti Niemi and Grant Murray combine to foil Marc Librra of Hibs during the Edinburgh derby

Ronald de Boer of Rangers gets the better of Kilmarnock's Freddie Dindeleux

something to celebrate, as Larsson later collected the Scottish Football Writers' Player of the Year Award while Martin O'Neill was named Manager of the Year.

While these presentations were taking place, Hearts and Hibs drew 0–0 at Tynecastle. This kept Hearts hot on the tail of Kilmarnock, who had crumbled to a 5–1 defeat at Ibrox 24 hours earlier in what was Ally McCoist's last appearance at the ground where he had had his greatest days. Killie boss Bobby Williamson was in no mood for sentiment and refused to bring McCoist on from the bench, but Rangers boss Dick Advocaat did get the legend on to the field, pushing him there to take his deserved bow at the end of the game.

It was also time for St Mirren to say goodbye – despite beating Aberdeen 2–1 at Love Street, they lost their SPL place as Dundee United came from behind to win 3–2 at McDiarmid Park. Meanwhile, Dunfermline and Motherwell saw out the penultimate fixture of their season, the Steelmen winning 2–1 at East End Park.

And so, after ten long months and 37 games, the final day of the League season was reached on Sunday, 20 May. It was marked by a minute's silence before the action could get under way, as a mark of respect for Lisbon Lion Bobby Murdoch who had died five days earlier.

When the referees' whistles did blow to start the games, it was Kilmarnock who proved the big

Motherwell's Steven Hammell, in action here against St Mirren

St Mirren manager Tom Hendrie finishes the season a disappointed man when his side fails to beat the drop, but he will aim to have the Buddies back in the big time before long

Motherwell's Stuart Elliott tries an overhead kick which brings a grimace to the face of St Johnstone defender Darren Dods

winners. They faced a weakened Celtic side at Rugby Park but were not in any mood to be easy on their visitors as victory would guarantee them a UEFA Cup spot. And they duly grabbed the opportunity with both hands, Alan Mahood scoring the only goal of the game to steal the thunder from Ally McCoist, who then hung up his boots after a glorious career. His previous club, Rangers, also signed off in style, hammering Hibs 4–0 at Ibrox in a day filled with emotion as Jorg Albertz and Tugay took their final bows before moving on to other clubs.

St Mirren said their farewell to the SPL with a 3–3 draw at Motherwell, while Dundee United gave their fans something else to cheer about as they concluded their troubled campaign with a 2–1 home win over Aberdeen.

Hearts, too, were last-day winners, defeating Dundee 2–0, while Dunfermline and St Johnstone were happy it was all over after finishing 0–0 at East End Park.

SCOTTISH PREMIER LEAGUE CHAMPIONSHIP 2000–1

	P	W	D	L	F	A	Pt
CELTIC	38	31	4	3	90	29	97
RANGERS	38	26	4	8	76	36	82
HIBERNIAN	38	18	12	8	57	35	66
KILMARNOCK	38	15	9	14	44	53	54
HEART OF MIDLOTHIAN	38	14	10	14	56	50	52
DUNDEE	38	13	8	17	51	49	47
ABERDEEN	38	11	12	15	45	52	45
MOTHERWELL	38	12	7	19	42	56	43
DUNFERMLINE ATHLETIC	38	11	9	18	34	54	42
ST JOHNSTONE	38	9	13	16	40	56	40
DUNDEE UNITED	38	9	8	21	38	63	35
ST MIRREN	38	8	6	24	32	72	30

Arthur Numan of Rangers battles to get past Ranko Popovic of Sturm Graz

RANGERS OFF TO A FLYER IN EUROPE

RANGERS had high hopes of making a major impact in the Champions League and got their campaign off to a flyer at Ibrox. In one of the club's best European performances for years, Dick Advocaat's side hammered Austrian side Sturm Graz 5–0.

It was as close to the perfect European display as you could have seen and filled the fans with massive optimism for the rest of the section. The key men on the famous night were Dutch masters Ronald de Boer, Michael Mols and Giovanni van Bronckhorst. Afterwards, van Bronckhorst praised de Boer and Mols after the £9m duo destroyed the Austrian champions.

'I felt they played really well together in what was just their second match as a partnership,' he said. 'Ronald did brilliantly to set up Michael for the first goal, chasing a ball that most people would have let run out. And it was a great twist and turn from Michael on the wing that led to Ronald's goal.

'I'm sure the more games they play together the more we will see them linking up. They are both fantastic players with great skills, and they can also score goals, which is crucial.

'It's great to see Michael back. I don't think we could put a price on how much we missed him last season. He brings a new dimension to the team, but we also have Billy Dodds in great form – his goal was as good as you would have seen anywhere in the Champions League last night.'

Van Bronckhorst's wasn't too bad either, a stinging drive for Rangers' fourth goal after great build-up play from de Boer.

'I thought Ronnie might go himself,' he added, 'but he slipped the ball to me and I made a great connection. I'm scoring a few goals right now from outside the box, and the more the better! I always try to get forward and help the strikers, and I knew when I hit the shot it was going in.

'It was a fantastic performance from the whole Rangers team because every side in the Champions League deserves to be there. Sturm Graz are not a bad side, we just played very well. And when we are in that form at Ibrox, I think we would give most teams a lot of problems.

'It was vital to get off to a winning start in our first home game. Last season we took just one point from the first two group matches, but already we have three from just one game.'

However, van Bronckhorst knew that much sterner tests lie ahead, with an away double-header against Monaco and Galatasaray to come next.

'We go to France next week and that will be a very difficult game. I know they are not in the best form, but the thing about the Champions League is that a win gets you right back in it, and that'll be the way they will be viewing the game against Rangers. They have some class players, and it will take a performance as good as last night's if we are to get something in Monaco. But we go there with confidence. I think we are growing in the Champions League, we have learned what it takes, and we must use that in the rest of the group matches.'

The Rangers campaign had started in some style, their best performance of a troubled season.

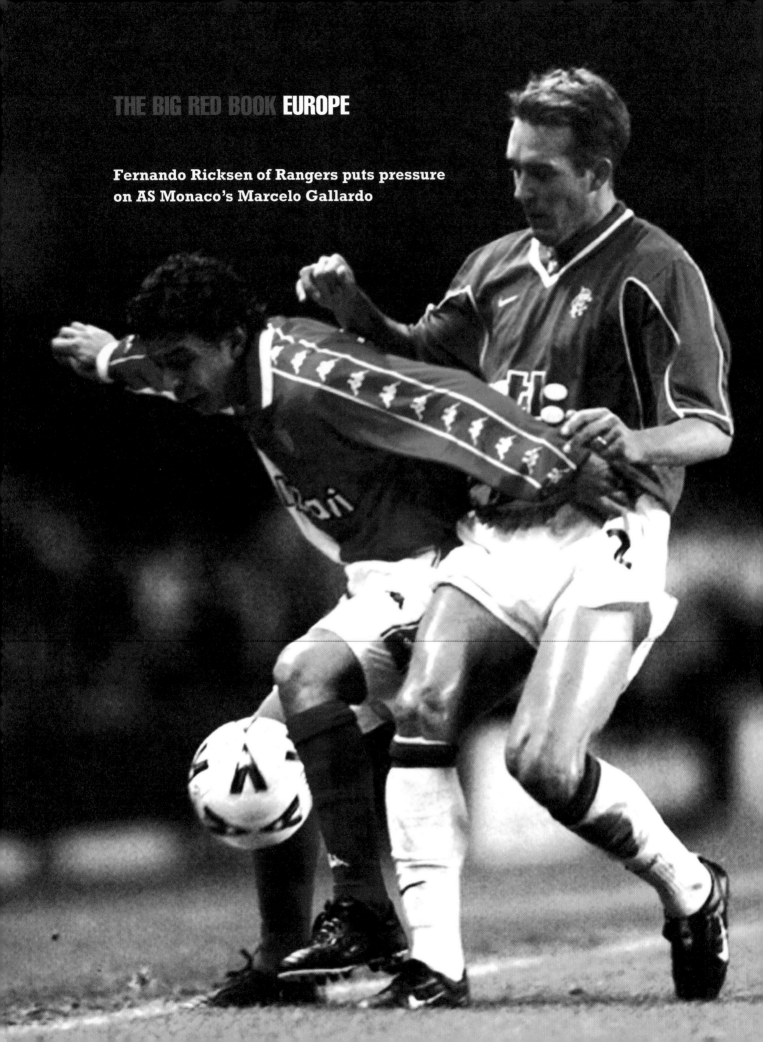

Fernando Ricksen of Rangers puts pressure on AS Monaco's Marcelo Gallardo

EUROPE

DREAM THAT TURNED NIGHTMARE

Europe remains the great unconquered continent for Scottish clubs after yet another season of disappointment in the UEFA Cup and Champions League. The days when our top clubs could progress through the early stages of the two competitions are but a dim and distant memory. And little was achieved on foreign fields last season to increase our credibility in European terms. In fact, it proved to be something of a disaster.

Yet, after the opening two games of their Champions League group, Rangers had appeared to be bang on course to change all that. They had demolished Austrian club Sturm Graz 5–0 at Ibrox in the opening tie, with goals from Michael Mols, Billy Dodds, Ronald De Boer, Jorg Albertz and Giovanni van Bronckhorst lighting up the packed ground and firing up the hopes of everyone at the club.

One week later, and those expectation levels were raised even higher when they went for bust in Monte Carlo and defeated Monaco 1–0. While Tugay's performance as sweeper captured many of the headlines, it was again van Bronckhorst who mattered in front of goal, or at least some 25 yards out, which was from where he launched his amazing winning shot. That victory put Rangers firmly in the driving seat at the top of their group, with Sturm Graz, Monaco and Turkish side Galatasaray trailing in their wake.

Rangers had easily qualified for this lucrative stage by overcoming Lithuanian minnows Zalgiris Kaunus 4–1 at home and then finishing the job with a goalless draw in the return leg. The final hurdle between them and the competition proper was Danish side Herfolge, but they too were dismissed with consummate ease. Rangers cruised to a 3–0 first leg win in Scandinavia before repeating the scoreline at Ibrox.

All this augured well for their chances in the group stages. And, with six points from two games, Dick Advocaat's previous disappointments at

Giovanni van Bronckhorst smashes home a 25-yarder against Monaco

failing to get his side beyond the first group stage were on course to be consigned to the dustbin.

Or so it seemed. Unfortunately, the bottom was about to fall out of their world, and Rangers would not stop falling all season. The first signs of trouble came in Istanbul, where Galatasaray raced to a 3–0 lead before Andrei Kanchelskis and van Bronckhorst restored some pride for the visitors with late goals. But, with Monaco winning 5–0 against Sturm Graz on the same evening, at least Rangers were still top of the group. And a victory at home against the Turks in their next game would have been enough to see them through.

Backed by a full house at Ibrox, it appeared an achievable target, but after 90 goalless minutes, it was the red-and-yellow-clad players who were smiling as the group opened up once again after Sturm Graz's 2–0 win over Monaco. And the Austrians, who had been viewed as the weakest team in the group before a ball had been kicked – an opinion given credence by their opening 5–0 defeat at Ibrox – were to

> **That did nothing to ease the pain felt as Rangers returned knowing it was all or nothing**

complete their turnaround in form and fortune by beating Rangers 2–0. The defeat was made all the harder to accept for Rangers as Arthur Numan had been sent off after collecting a second booking for allegedly returning to the field without permission after receiving treatment. The decision was ludicrous, as the referee could clearly be seen to wave him back on, and the red card was overturned at a later appeal. But that did nothing to ease the pain felt as Rangers returned from Austria knowing it was now all or nothing against Monaco in the final game of the group. They knew they had to win to go through, and twice they led as a result of goals from Kenny Miller and then Michael Mols.

But Monaco were also walking a qualification tightrope, and they hit back twice to tie the game, their second and ultimately fatal equaliser coming just 12 minutes from time. In the final shakedown, the result put both teams out of the Champions League as Galatasaray and Sturm Graz emerged from their game in Turkey with the same scoreline

Catch me if you can . . . Kenny Miller celebrates his opener against Monaco in the final game of the group

Michael Mols is in heaven after making it 2–1 for Rangers

and the point apiece they needed to finish first and second in the table.

Like the rest of his team-mates, Michael Mols was distraught after the implications of the results had sunk in.

'The goals we lost were poor,' he said. 'We gave it our best shot, but the draw wasn't enough. If you look at the results, then we didn't deserve to go through, but if you look at the game, we had enough chances, so I have mixed feelings.'

Arthur Numan agreed that they had shot themselves in the foot.

'Against a team like Monaco,' he said, 'it's important not to give away clear chances. We couldn't win our home games against Galatasaray and Monaco. I would have expected us to get a victory in at least one of them, and to miss out again is a huge blow for the whole club. But we just have to get on with it.'

Which meant a drop down to the UEFA Cup third round. But more misery awaited Rangers there, when Kaiserslautern recovered from losing Jurgen Pettersen and 1–0 at Ibrox to a late Albertz goal, progressing to the fourth round with a 3–0 demolition job back in Germany.

Penalty! Henrik Larsson wins a penalty in Bordeaux

Celtic's Jackie McNamara gets the better of the Bordeaux defence

Celtic utility player Jackie McNamara in European action against Jeunesse Esch

For Advocaat's men, Europe was over for another year. Their only consolation was that they had lasted a month longer than any of the other Scottish hopefuls. Celtic had crashed out in the second round of the UEFA Cup to Bordeaux. Martin O'Neill's men had returned from France with a creditable 1–1 draw, their goal earned by Henrik Larsson, who was brought down for the penalty he converted himself.

When Lubo Moravcik gave Celtic the lead in the return at Parkhead, they appeared to be on their way to the third round. But lanky Lilian Laslandes had other ideas. He fired in an equaliser to stun the home crowd seven minutes from time and take the game into extra time. Then he struck again in the added 30 minutes to leave Celtic shell-shocked and out. The Parkhead side had

progressed to that stage with an effortless 11–0 aggregate demolition of Luxembourg side Jeunesse Esche, the 4–0 away win followed by a 7–0 thrashing at Celtic Park, the highlight of which was a three-minute hat-trick from Mark Burchill, regarded as the fastest ever in European competition. That would have given first-round opponents HJK Helsinki food for thought, but they still could not stop Larsson scoring twice to give Celtic a decent advantage to take to Finland.

Unfortunately for Martin O'Neill and his side, they were in for a shock even before the ball was kicked. The playing surface in Helsinki was described by the Celtic boss as the worst he had ever seen. The damage had been done by pop fans crowding on to the pitch for a Tina Turner concert a few days earlier. Huge holes created by

Disappointment in Europe for Aberdeen's manager, Ebbe Skovdahl, when his team fails to get through the qualifying round

Stuttgart's Pablo Thiam gets away from Heart's Colin Cameron

the stage had been filled in and covered with patches of artificial turf. So it was no surprise that Celtic's normal passing game proved ineffective. After 90 minutes they found themselves 2–0 down, putting the tie into extra time. That was the signal for Chris Sutton to score his first European goal for the club and see them safely through to face Bordeaux.

While Celtic progressed to the second round, Hearts fell foul of Stuttgart – literally. The Germans were reduced to nine men at Tynecastle but still managed to limit the capital side to a 3–2 victory, with goals from defenders Steven Pressley and Gordan Petric plus a penalty from Colin Cameron. On the back of Stuttgart's 1–0 win in the first leg, that was good enough to carry them through on the away-goals rule.

Hearts had good cause to feel an injustice had been done but ultimately recognised that they had only themselves to blame for failing to adequately hammer home their numerical advantage at Tynecastle. If they had been half as clinical in front of goal as they had been in the qualifying round

against Icelandic side IBV, they would have remained in the competition. They won 2–0 in Iceland before finishing the job in style with a 3–0 win at Tynecastle. But at least they could go out with their heads held high – unlike Aberdeen.

The one-time Cup-Winners' Cup and Super Cup winners sank to an all-time low when they were dumped from the qualifying round by Bohemians of Dublin. The writing was on the wall when they lost the first leg 2–1 in front of a stunned home crowd, who had thought they would be watching another minnow side put to the sword. At least Robbie Winters' goal gave them some hope to cling to as they headed across the Irish Sea for the return. But not even an own goal by ten-man Bohemians' David Morrison could save them, and they went out on the away-goals rule. Chairman Stewart Milne faced calls for his resignation when he returned to the Granite City. In a strange twist, however, manager Ebbe Skovdahl gave the chairman his vote of confidence, which just about summed up how upside-down Aberdeen's European credibility had become.

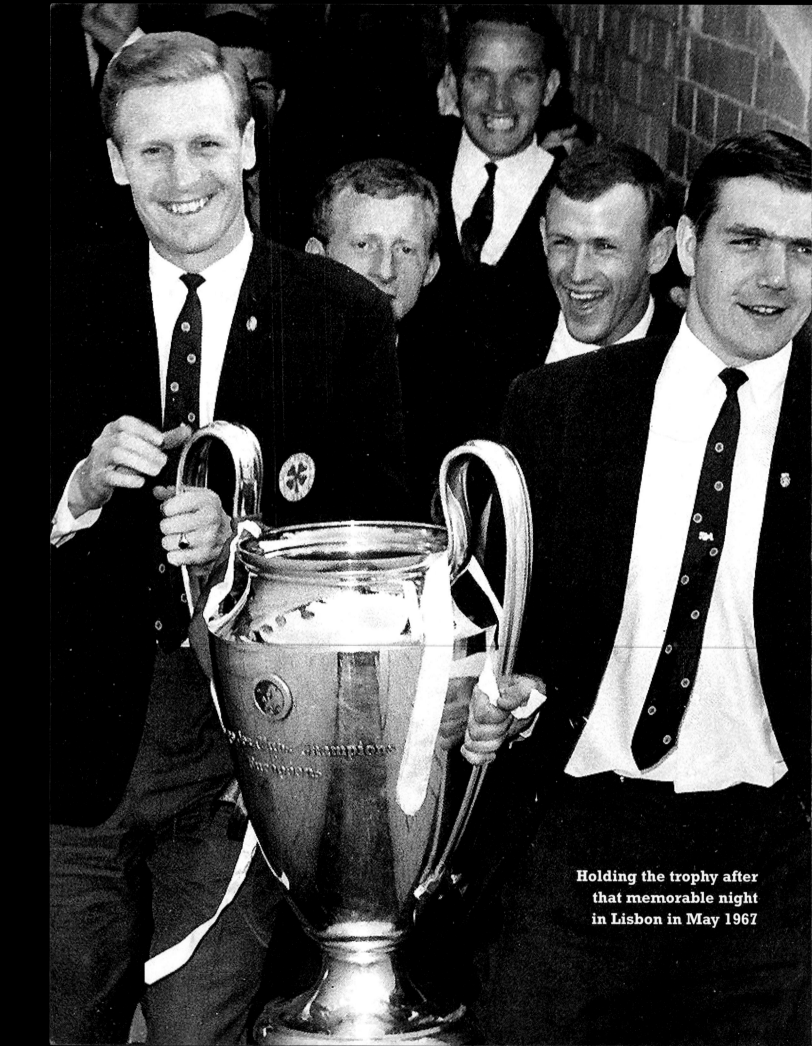

Holding the trophy after that memorable night in Lisbon in May 1967

BILLY McNEILL
A GENUINE CHAMPION

FOREVER, in football terms anyway, Billy McNeill will be recalled as the first British footballer to hold aloft the European Cup. Yet that glorious night in Lisbon in May 1967, when Celtic beat Inter Milan 2–1, has a contender for personal gratification. Fifteen years later the man who was the late Jock Stein's on-field general emerged as the club's commander-in-chief in one of their most celebrated European successes.

Tonight, at the Amsterdam Arena, Celtic will face Ajax in the first leg of the third qualifying round, the prize for the two matches translating into a place in the initial group stages of the Champions League proper. As McNeill watches, he will recall that autumn evening all those years ago. He has collected many major prizes during his managerial career, most notably the double of Scottish Premiership Champions and Scottish Cup in his second spell at Parkhead in 1988 and, earlier, promotion from the then English Second Division with Manchester City. But high on his list of great memories is the 2–1 win over Ajax on their own turf in 1982. McNeill – who had taken over from Stein in '78 in football's equivalent of a third world *coup d'état* engineered by the late chairman Desmond White – had restored a vibrancy and self-belief in Celtic, guiding them to three championships out of four in his initial spell in charge.

When the European Cup first round draw was made – and there was no seeding or country co-efficient status in those take-it-or-leave-it times – Celtic were paired with Ajax, whose dominance of the business may have slipped marginally at the time yet they still remained awesome. Johan Cruyff was on a double-shift, managing the club he had graced so eloquently and continuing to damage opponents on the field. The odds were definitely against Celtic, especially as Ajax had strolled through the first leg in Glasgow and had returned across the North Sea with a 2–2 draw that should have been a victory.

The tie had ostensibly been done and dusted, but Cruyff and Ajax had failed to do their homework on McNeill. Just as he had led Celtic to their ultimate European triumph in '67, so he would again confound the odds stacked before them now. Even today he will readily proclaim the return match at Amsterdam's Olympic Stadium to be a stellar moment in his managerial career. Celtic won by 2–1, one of the most adventurous goals of Charlie Nicholas' career being followed by a last-minute strike by George McCluskey.

As he had been in Lisbon, McNeill was king for a day or two. But the then Celtic board were not known for their loyalty. Managers were treated as serfs, as Stein had discovered when he was summarily and disgracefully shown the exit and offered a job running the club pools division. McNeill didn't last long, decamping to Manchester after a dispute over the paltry wages he was paid.

He has always enjoyed a powerful sense of loyalty, however. This dragged him back to Celtic for the club's centenary year and he is justifiably proud of the fact that he overcame the massive wealth that had been injected into Rangers. But that night in Amsterdam probably consumes him and rests proudly alongside the earlier European Cup triumph.

'I knew we must have done something right,' he said at the time, 'because afterwards big Desmond [White] bought champagne in the hotel for both the players and the back-room staff, and that truly is a one-off.'

As fierce a competitor as you would wish to find, and with a track record for Celtic and Scotland confirming his intensity of spirit, McNeill is also a genuine hands-up guy. He has always despised defeat but, when the angst drips off him, he can rationalise and seek out the causes and reasons. Nor is he ever slow in giving praise wherever it is due.

Tonight, when Celtic take the field in Amsterdam, the memories of grand times will return. Celtic will have a passionate supporter and an outstanding man in their corner – albeit subliminally.

TRUE BLUE BARRY

Rangers' captain
Barry Ferguson
brushes aside
Colin Cameron
of Hearts

TRUE BLUE BARRY

In a season of gloom, one shining light continued to sparkle for Rangers. Barry Ferguson is the beacon that continued to burn brightly at the end of what was a very long, dark tunnel.

He has emerged from season 2000–1 without any medals but with a bucketful of experience that can only help him realise the potential he has shown since breaking into the Rangers first team as a teenager. Now, at the age of 23, he is widely acknowledged by team-mates and opponents alike to be the finest midfield player Scotland has produced for a generation.

The men who managed him last season, Dick Advocaat at Rangers and Craig Brown at international level, don't agree on much, but they are in accord over the quality of Ferguson. So much so, that Advocaat handed Fergie the ultimate honour any Rangers player could attain when he made him club captain back in October 2000.

The armband may be light, but the responsibility weighs heavy, and the appointment has helped Ferguson to emerge as a dominant force in the Scottish game. Craig Brown even foresees future Scotland teams being built around the precocious talent that lurks behind the baby face.

Barry is an outstanding person, typical of the great players of the past

'Barry is an outstanding person, typical of the great players of the past. He comes from the West of Scotland, and when we look at the number of foreigners who are now in our game, I reckon he has shown that Scottish talent is still available. I just wish there was much more.' For now, however, Brown is just grateful we have Fergie, who has already confirmed his arrival on the international stage with accomplished performances against some of the top midfielders in the world.

At club level, too, he has more than held his own when competing in the European arena, drawing praise from opponents with the same ease and regularity he finds a team-mate with a pass. Unfortunately, the captain's armband is all that Ferguson has to show for a season of endeavour. He had hoped to see silver at the end of his rainbow, but instead all he saw was a myriad of red and yellow as his enthusiasm to achieve erred on the side of over-exuberance.

The Rangers fans may have appreciated his extra effort, but the referees certainly did not. Two red cards and 15 yellows underline that fact. A nagging rib injury that hampered him throughout the final few months of a difficult campaign only added injury to insult as Fergie finally had to concede that he could do no more to prevent a trophyless season.

But from every bad experience comes some good, and the man who carries the hopes of all Rangers' fans on his shoulders refuses to be downhearted for long. With a little help from his friends, Ferguson believes he can lift trophies for the Ibrox club, and he is convinced he has the

support he needs to join the ranks of men like John Greig, Terry Butcher and Richard Gough as successful leaders of Rangers.

'Since I was appointed captain at the end of October,' he explained, 'the experienced players have been great. I wasn't certain about how they would react to a younger guy being given the job, but they have allowed me to get on with things and have backed me 100 per cent. I know that if I need any help it is there for me. The likes of Arthur Numan are always available, as is manager Dick Advocaat.'

Numan and Advocaat were always there for Fergie when things were not going so well last season. His disciplinary record was in danger of overwhelming him at one point as he accumulated

Barry Ferguson with Lubomir Moravcik in an Old Firm clash

Captain Ferguson nets a gem against their old rivals

bookings and sendings-off faster than Rangers accumulated points. But all along he insisted, 'I'm no bad boy. Suddenly I'm being branded Scotland's dirtiest player, and that's not fair. Yes, I picked up a few bookings, but a lot of them were harsh. I've never set out to deliberately hurt someone, that's just not my style. A lot of my tackles have been mistimed, and that's a part of my game I'll work on.'

Despite this trouble with officialdom, Ferguson continued to catch the eye of more than referees. Arsenal, Leeds, Liverpool and Chelsea were all credited with an interest in luring him South of the Border, while a handful of Europe's leading clubs were also hot on his trail throughout the year, alerted by a star showing throughout Rangers' Champions League and UEFA Cup campaigns. Such attention quickly saw a £10m price tag

pinned to his head, all of which would be enough to dazzle many a wide-eyed youngster.

But Ferguson remains focused on his future and is happy to play for the club he has supported since childhood.

'I've three years left on my contract, and I've no intention of leaving,' he insisted. 'I will honour that. I am very proud to be captain of Rangers, and I am not going anywhere. My dream has always been to play for Rangers and be captain – why would I want to leave?'

Numan for one is delighted to hear him talk such sense. The Dutchman has played with some of Europe's top players, and he claimed, 'No one at this club has impressed me more than Barry. He is an exceptional talent, and I believe that, for the next few years anyway, he should continue to play in Scotland with Rangers. It is all too easy for a

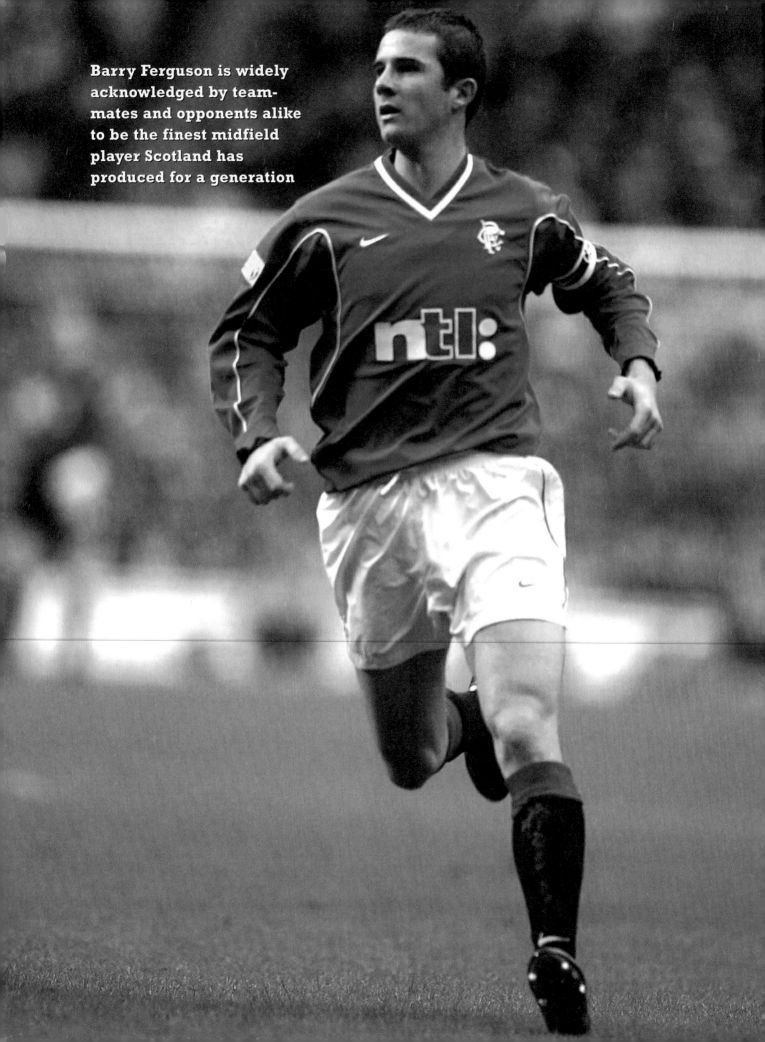

Barry Ferguson is widely acknowledged by team-mates and opponents alike to be the finest midfield player Scotland has produced for a generation

Barry Ferguson scores in the 5–1 win over Celtic

youngster to be lured to the leagues in Italy, Spain or England and, at times, such moves hinder their progress.

'When I was 21 and playing in Holland for Twente Enschede,' he continued, 'I was set for a move to Manchester City. All the negotiations had been completed, and I had even travelled to Manchester to speak with their manager at the time, Peter Reid. But I rethought the plans and decided to stay in Holland. It was there that I learned how to play football. Some seven years later I moved on to PSV Eindhoven where Dick Advocaat was manager, and there is no doubt that this learning process within my home country has been of great benefit. It can be difficult for a young man to move outwith his own culture. It is much better to grow up within your country and with your friends before you venture abroad. Barry has a wonderful football future, and I know the manager rates him highly. He has to remember that he is just 23, so to even think about moving clubs at this age would be a bad move in my opinion.'

Not even an agonising season such as the one just past can undermine Fergie's determination to keep his feet firmly on home soil and help put Rangers back on top. When he says the campaign left him hurting, he means that literally. The rib injury he struggled to play with towards the final few weeks finally took their toll and cost him a

couple of caps against Poland and San Marino in the process. Not even regular visits to an oxygen chamber could relieve the pain.

As he whiled away the hours recovering, he could have been forgiven for allowing his mind to pick the bones out of a season that had promised so much. The recurring theme was injury to key players, including himself. This cost Rangers the chance to progress into the second group stage of the Champions League after a Ferguson-inspired first few games had appeared to open the door for them.

The damage was not limited to Europe, however, as the battle on the home front was also badly undermined by the growing list of casualties. There was at least some respite from the onslaught when Rangers turned the tables on Celtic and avenged their early-season 6–2 defeat at Parkhead with a 5–1 victory at Ibrox in November. It was doubly sweet for Fergie, as he opened the scoring that day with a goal that owed nothing to luck and everything to skill and composure.

'In November,' said Fergie, 'when we beat Celtic 5–1, we played them off the park. So we know we have the ability to play like that.'

And, as Rangers continue to ring the changes in their pursuit of the glories that evaded them last season, Ferguson remains the fulcrum around which all things good will revolve.

Ramon Vega in an airborne battle with Alan Mahood and Kevin McGowne in the Celtic v. Kilmarnock CIS Insurance League Cup final

FIRST TASTE OF SILVERWARE

The CIS Insurance League Cup was not high on Martin O'Neill's list of priorities when he took over as manager of Celtic, but it will forever hold a place in his heart after it became the first piece of silverware the Hoops lifted under his stewardship.

As such, it was the first major block in the building of the treble, and it underlined once and for all that his side were not only good – they were also winners. None more so than striker Henrik Larsson, who scored a glorious hat-trick that left Kilmarnock's players as breathless as the 52,000 fans who packed into Hampden to witness it. By contrast, the Swede's striking partner, Chris Sutton, made the headlines for all the wrong reasons. His challenge on Gary Holt on the hour mark brought an instant red card.

As it was, his departure merely served to galvanise his ten remaining team-mates, who had already bounced back from the loss of Bobby Petta through injury after only 12 minutes of the final. Like Sutton, who had been nursing a shoulder injury going into the Hampden showdown, Petta had been battling for weeks before this to overcome a troublesome problem – in his case affecting his groin. But the Dutch winger's delight at making it on to the pitch was short-lived. In fact, 12 seconds was all it took for the first crunching tackle to leave him writhing in agony. As he had done for the weeks leading up to this, Celtic physio Brian Scott managed to patch him up once more. But Petta's final was clearly going to be a brief affair, and young Stephen Crainey soon found himself thrown into the action as a replacement.

Already in the Celtic line-up was another wonder Bhoy, Colin Healy, as experienced pair Jackie McNamara and Alan Thompson were ruled out by suspension while Didier Agathe and Rab Douglas were ineligible as they were cup-tied. None of this upset the script, which dictated that it was going to be Celtic's day. They had won the same trophy the previous season, even without Larsson who was then nursing a broken leg. But that success was little more than a day of

The beginning of the end for Kilmarnock as Henrik Larsson opens the scoring

Henrik Larsson (left) slots home his second past the helpless Kilmarnock goalkeeper Gordon Marshall

Henrik Larsson completes his hat-trick in the League Cup final by rounding Gordon Marshall and slotting the ball home

sanctuary in a season of misery. This time, lifting the CIS League Cup was to officially herald the dawn of a new era, and the man to deliver the goods was Super Swede Larsson. He not only broke Killie's hearts with his hat-trick, he also shattered any lingering doubts that Celtic's bubble was about to burst after the teams had gone in at the interval without a goal between them. Larsson put that right three minutes after the restart, when a Moravcik cross came off the chest of Ramon Vega and fell perfectly for the deadly striker to hammer home.

Any hope Killie had of hauling themselves back into the game after Sutton's dismissal was blown away by Larsson's second after 74 minutes. Young Killie defender Chris Innes believed he had done enough to shut the striker down, but Larsson's shot simply flew off his outstretched foot and looped past the helpless Gordon Marshall.

If that had a touch of luck about it, Larsson's third, ten minutes from time, had a touch of class. He collected the ball inside his own half, ran through an involuntarily parting Killie defence before shimmying to send Marshall down and advancing to slip the ball into the empty net for what he later described as his best goal of the season.

The headlines were Larsson's, the Cup was Celtic's, the treble was on. As usual, the modest Larsson, still sporting his sprig of lucky white heather, chose to ignore his own contribution and instead praised his team-mates, who had refused to be distracted by the departure of Sutton.

'That just shows the character this team has,' he said. 'We never give up. We were 1–0 up when Chris was sent off, so that made it a bit easier. But we fought for each other, and nobody wanted to give up. That's why we won 3–0.'

'I was in the stand last year,' he continued, 'and watched the final from there, so I was pleased to have the chance to play this time. It's a big moment, a big win. Now this is in the bag, we have to focus on winning the League.'

While Larsson and his team-mates moved on to bigger things, Killie were left to lick their wounds. None more so than Ian Durrant, who had gambled on being able to play through an injury to take part in the final but lost in more ways than one as yet another career-threatening problem forced him out of the action.

At least he had got to the final. His former club,

Rangers, had fallen at the penultimate hurdle when they were defeated 3–1 by Larsson-led Celtic. The Swede grabbed two of his side's goals, one from the penalty spot, before a packed Hampden crowd, while Sutton knocked in the other. Jorg Albertz had done his best to give Rangers hope by converting a penalty, but the match will be best – or worst – remembered for a massive flare-up in the dying minutes following a challenge by Claudio Reyna on Bobby Petta, which resulted in the American, Michael Mols and Lubo Moravcik all being shown red cards by under-pressure ref Willie Young. When the dust had settled, it transpired that Reyna had actually received the equivalent of two red cards and three yellows during and after the match, all of which ruled Reyna, Mols and Moravcik out of the following Sunday's Old Firm League meeting at Celtic Park.

The explosion at Hampden had been in stark contrast to events at the national stadium 24 hours earlier, when Kilmarnock and St Mirren had met to decide which of them made it to the final. Only 9,000 hardy souls turned out to see that honour fall to Bobby Williamson's men, who swept past the Buddies 3–0 with goals from Andy McLaren, Craig Dargo and Peter Canero. In fact, after scraping past Clyde after extra time in the second round, Killie had to overcome an all-Premier route to the final, having defeated St Johnstone 1–0 in Perth in

Bobby Peta bursts beyond Claudio Reyna in Celtic's 3–1 semi-final victory over Rangers

Kilmarnock's Andy McLaren explodes on to the ball in the League Cup semi-final against St Mirren

the third round and Hibs 2–1 at Rugby Park in the quarter-final.

Teams involved in European competition were excused duty in the first two rounds, and Celtic's first involvement had seen them field against Raith Rovers a smattering of young players who still managed to delight the home crowd with a comprehensive 4–0 win. Their quarter-final, against Hearts at Tynecastle, had been a much closer affair as the fresh-faced Bhoys were held to

a 2–2 draw after 90 minutes before stepping up a gear to go through 5–2 after extra time.

Rangers had also used the early stages of the competition to give some fringe players a run-out but still managed to defeat Aberdeen 4–2 at Ibrox, then Dundee United 2–0 at the same venue. In fact, shocks were few and far between in the competition, with the Dumbarton team creating the only real upset in the opening round when removing Ayr in a penalty shoot-out.

Neil Lennon shows off the League Cup after his side's comprehensive win in the final

Slim Jim at
the height
of his career

SALUTE TO A LEGEND
JIM BAXTER, 1939–2001

SCOTTISH football paid an eloquent tribute to former Rangers and Scotland player Jim Baxter at Glasgow Cathedral today. Baxter's life was celebrated at the service and the great and good of football, politics and the arts turned up from every corner of the country and beyond. They were joined in huge numbers by those to whom Baxter felt most affinity – the supporters who adored him.

The service heard full tribute to the man who died on Saturday, 14 April 2001 at 61 from cancer. It was the quintessential reflection of his life and times – a capacity crowd, with many locked out but happy enough to observe the occasion from outside.

'He was a delight to be with both on the field and in the dressing room,' said Ralph Brand, former team-mate of the 1960s. 'When we played there was strict discipline at Rangers and when we had to appear at the top of the marble staircase at Ibrox to face the manager, Scot Symon, we were cracking in anticipation. But Jim always had his own ideas about authority – and didn't care too much for it. He was his own man.'

Brand went on to tell the story of how Baxter gathered his team-mates in the dressing room before a match. In those days the game was played with a laced ball, more difficult to control and pass than today's. That was never a problem.

'"How would you like the passes played today?" he'd ask. "With the lace in front of you or away from you?"' It was a bit of fun, but it was also half-serious because of the incredible self-belief he had in his talents.

Baxter's off-field exploits have been well documented, but there was a side to him that didn't involve flash cars, expensive suits and trendy night-clubs. This was illuminated by Baxter's close friend, Scots author William McIlvanney, whom he'd asked to say a few words.

'He had feet of gold laced with diamonds, but he'd claim they were feet of clay. Jim was a very self-critical man and one of his greatest attributes was that he took total responsibility for his own actions throughout his life.

'Watching him in his prime on a football field must have been like getting a season ticket to Nirvana. In 1963 and 1967, when he played those outstanding games for Scotland against England, Jim owned Wembley. In the second of those matches, when Scotland beat the World Champions, his attitude was to show them who could really play. Scotland won by 3–2, but in Jim's view we massacred them by one goal.'

The service included Bible readings by Baxter's son, Allan, and by Chancellor of the Exchequer Gordon Brown, who had sold programmes at Baxter's first senior club, Raith Rovers. He once said to Baxter that it was ridiculous he was transferred to Rangers for £16,500, to which came the reply: 'You're the Chancellor and you can't get your arithmetic right. They paid £17,500 for me.'

Baxter's great gift was to cross the West of Scotland divide. He was a Rangers man, but his talent and style earned him a special place in the thoughts of Celtic fans, past and present. Many of them stood, heads bowed, outside of the cathedral. At the end a lone piper from his Army regiment, the Black Watch, played 'A Scottish Soldier'. Nothing could have been more appropriate for the memory of a man who would take on anybody, anytime and anywhere.

Dick Advocaat had his
troubles last season as
his team lost form and
were plagued by injuries

THE BIG RED BOOK **DICK ADVOCAAT**

DICK ADVOCAAT

Dick Advocaat is known as a superb tactician, respected as an excellent man-manager and feared as someone who will accept nothing less than 100 per cent from those he works with. But above all else he is a winner, and that's why the events of season 2000–1 hurt him badly – very badly.

Since arriving at Ibrox from PSV Eindhoven in the summer of 1998, winning has been not only his yardstick but his trademark. Rangers benefited, as he got the club back on track after a hiccup at the end of Walter Smith's reign. Then their bid for ten championships in a row was halted by Celtic and they finished the season without a trophy for the first time since before the Graeme Souness revolution took place back in 1986. Advocaat made it business as usual by wresting the SPL trophy back from the Parkhead club and adding the League Cup and Scottish Cups in a debut season that confirmed that Rangers' future was in safe hands.

It was accepted by all who follow the fortunes of the club, therefore, that it would be the same

An excellent man-manager and feared as someone who will accept nothing less than 100 per cent from those he works with

again the following season. And so it almost proved, with only the League Cup slipping out of Advocaat's firm grasp and denying him the elusive back-to-back trebles – a feat not yet achieved by any manager in Scotland.

Nevertheless, five out of six trophies in his first two years convinced Rangers' fans that Advocaat's strict, disciplined approach and determination to succeed would keep the good times rolling. So, when the wheels came off the bandwagon big style last season, the thump was felt by all. None more so than Advocaat, who, for the first time since arriving on these shores, felt the cold chill of criticism.

This was a man who had managed and coached at the highest level with club and country. Even when he was operating in the rarefied atmosphere of the 1994 World Cup finals in America with Holland, his standards dictated that he was there to win, and it took the wonderful Brazilian side of that year to see his Dutch side off the premises.

Dick Advocaat and John Greig watch pensively as the action unfolds on the field of play

But even a master of his craft like Advocaat can't work without the tools of his trade. And, amid scenes more appropriate to a hospital emergency room, he found himself surrounded by wounded heroes almost for the duration of last season. Injuries can be coped with, but this was carnage.

'Last season, some people were out for more games than they played, and it is impossible to have a good team when people are in and out all the time,' insists Advocaat. 'This season, if everyone stays fit, I will not need to bring in a lot of new players.'

It was not just numbers that concerned Advocaat as he attempted to keep pace-setting Celtic in his sights during the first few months of last season. Key personnel, like Michael Mols, Craig Moore and Giovanni van Bronckhorst, were falling like ninepins. The heart of his side was being ripped asunder. Worse still, those who were left standing were not always performing with the

> **Amid scenes more appropriate to a hospital emergency room, he found himself surrounded by wounded heroes**

grit and determination the manager demands.

After one particularly unacceptable defeat at McDiarmid Park, Advocaat's top finally blew. Accusing some of his players of being 'bigheads', he left no one in any doubt that he considered they were spending too much time on their Internet websites and golf courses. Like a wounded animal, he came out snarling. But not even this demonstration of emotion and passion from the manager could patch together a season that was rapidly disintegrating for Rangers.

'Footballers know when they have a bad season, and everyone at the club realises they cannot hide from what happened,' admits Advocaat.

Despite all the agonies – physical and mental – endured by all at Ibrox, however, the Dutchman never lost sight of the fact that his job – indeed his vocation – is to get Rangers right back up there again. Walking away is never an option for him. And, with his inner confidence undented, that's precisely where he aims to put them, taking the first few steps to recovery towards the end of the season when his side started to welcome back several recovering stars who helped finish the season on a winning note.

Even in his darkest hour, Advocaat fought hard to retain a philosophical approach and admitted, 'I like to win every game, but this is the sort of time that every manager gets at some point. For two and a half years everything was good, everybody was happy, we won a lot of games and did well in Europe. Now we are in a period where not everything is going the right way. But I have that at home with my wife, as well.'

A rare glimpse of the well-hidden sense of humour from a man who doesn't believe ten words are necessary when two will do.

But at least there was some brief respite in a troubled season when Rangers delighted their fans by thumping Celtic 5–1 in a League clash at Ibrox in November. This helped to heal some of the wounds inflicted in the 6–2 defeat in their opening SPL meeting at Parkhead, but it did little to paper over the cracks, and Advocaat was realistic enough to recognise this fact.

The crushing blow they suffered when failing to qualify from their Champions League group was still being sorely felt, and already Advocaat knew he had a major job on his hands to stem the flow of silverware slipping through the club's fingers. But he is single-minded to the extent of being obsessed when it comes to achieving a goal. And his determination has remained to get Rangers back into a winning groove. Sometimes that can mean leaving out players who believe they should be given a first-team jersey and who, on occasion, even have the backing of the supporters in this belief. But, as Advocaat has insisted, 'In football the job of the head coach is to maximise the talents of the players he has available. I have never had favourites, and I have always selected the people I consider to be the most capable for a match. There are no personal issues involved in my decisions. At Rangers I, like every other manager, have had to make choices that may be unpopular with some. But that is my job, and I cannot allow myself to be distracted.'

And neither has he been, as a summer designed for rest and relaxation was transformed into a couple of months of high activity. The

rebuilding began, the refocusing continued. The recovery of Rangers was the priority. The reinstatement of Dick Advocaat as a winner must surely follow.

As he said, 'In the first two seasons we won five prizes and everything was okay, but now there is something to prove again, and I think that is a good thing for us.'

It's certainly a good thing for Rangers that Advocaat is the man ready to lead them back up that hill. With Jan Wouters now at his side, and with the very impressive Murray Park training complex at his disposal, Advocaat believes he is better placed than ever to get the best from his side. The addition of Claudio Caniggia, Christian Nerlinger, Russell Latapy, Michael Ball and Shota Aizveladze has ensured it is a new-look Rangers side that Advocaat sends out this year. But the ethos remains the same – be winners, just like the coach.

Dick Advocaat makes a point during a Rangers training session

Bobby Murdoch was
one of the greatest
midfielders ever to
have graced the Hoops

LEGEND WILL NEVER DIE
BOBBY MURDOCH, 1944–2001

THIS HAS BEEN a desperate year for those of us in Scotland who love our football heroes. The news of Bobby Murdoch's death on Tuesday, 15 May 2001 coming as it does just weeks after Jim Baxter passed away, is a huge and disheartening blow.

If Murdoch never quite attained the fame of Baxter, he was shoulder-to-shoulder with him in terms of his consummate skills, one of the most gifted midfielders the business has produced. Like Baxter, he was a footballer who thrived upon the challenge of the big occasion, and never more so than when, on a balmy night in Lisbon in 1967, he drove Celtic to their European Cup triumph over Inter Milan.

Murdoch was immense in the Portuguese capital, dominating a celebrated Italian midfield with his wonderful combination of touch, vision and sheer hardness. His nickname within Parkhead was 'Chopper'. When it got combative, Murdoch was right up alongside the very best of them. The likes of Dave Mackay, Norman Hunter, Nobby Stiles, Ron Harris and Billy Bremner were all more than capable of damaging opponents, but none of them fancied a face-to-face with Murdoch.

That European Cup final tour de force apart, Murdoch's alliance of skill and hardness was prominent, possibly decisive, during the two matches Celtic played against Leeds United in that famous European Cup semi-final tie at Elland Road and subsequently Hampden in 1970. Bremner, who by then had more or less taken over from Murdoch on the right side of the Scotland midfield, was dwarfed by his presence. Celtic qualified for the final after two epic games and, although they ultimately lost out to Feyenoord, the success over the then champions of England will forever be regarded by Celtic supporters as one of the club's major achievements.

Murdoch's special skill was in the co-ordination of his eye and his right foot. The very fact that in 484 games for Celtic between 1959 and 1973 he managed to score 105 goals underlines that point. The ratio is close to a goal in every four games, a quite remarkable statistic. Placed alongside his other attributes – his creativity and his willingness to scuffle – Murdoch was more or less the complete article.

His one failing – if it could be so termed – was a lack of pace. Then again, such a charge was also levelled at Baxter. Essentially, the two men did not require the speed of an Olympic sprint champion because their game revolved around that rare commodity: intelligence.

Incredibly, he won just 12 caps for Scotland, but that figure has to be placed in context because, in his prime, he had to contest the right midfield role with the likes of Mackay, Bremner, John Greig and Paddy Crerand. Stein, who was as fine a judge of a footballer as you could possibly have wished to find, regarded him as one of Celtic's truly significant operators.

'Bobby gave us a wonderful balance,' he once said. 'He could play short passes, long passes, score goals, defend, and also make his presence felt in a physical sense. He was an outstanding player for us and I think that his partnership with Bertie Auld in the middle of the field gave us the ideal balance. There is no doubt about it. Bobby was a major component of our successes in that era.'

Aged just 56, Murdoch's has been a short life in today's terms, yet it crammed many memorable moments into its time span. He was a top team player while still a teenager, and all the promise he showed when he scored in his début against Hearts was fulfilled over a memorable decade in the '60s.

The young man from Bothwell could never have envisaged the success he would enjoy or the great times he would share with a disparate collection of personalities at Parkhead. The medals he won tell something of the story. They reflect a superb career, but they don't really tell the story of a very quiet and mannerly man. He will be another big miss.

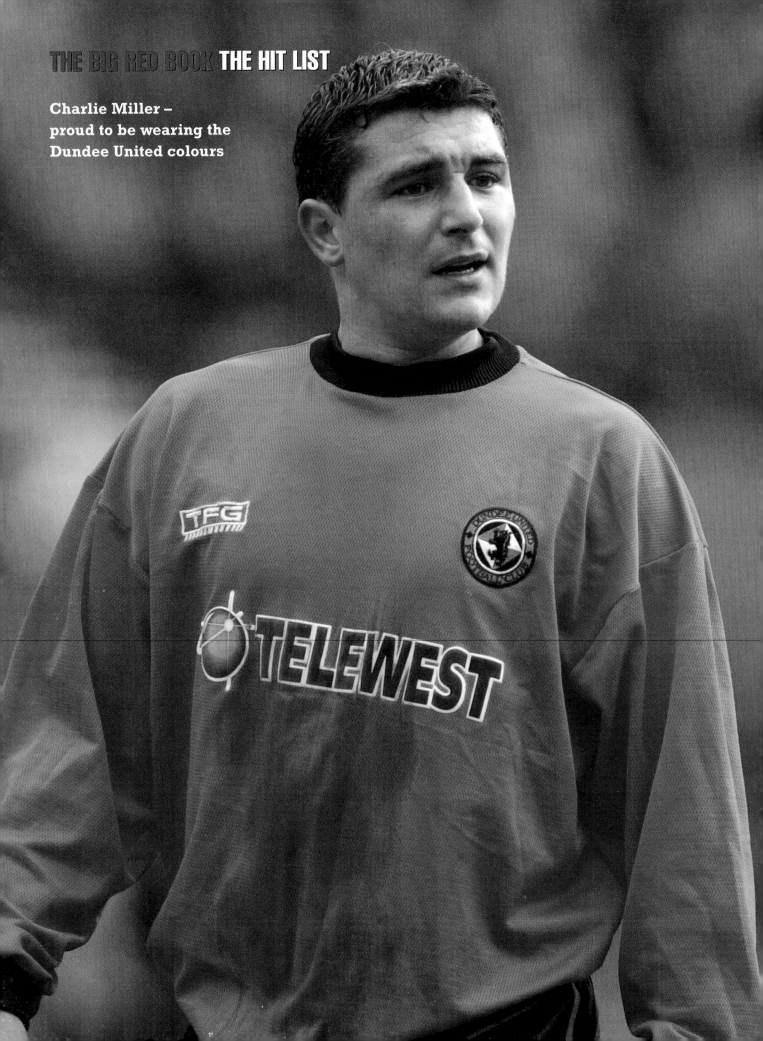

**Charlie Miller –
proud to be wearing the
Dundee United colours**

THE HIT LIST

Gavin Rae – 'worth £10 million'

GAVIN RAE DUNDEE

In an era when young Scottish talent is being muscled aside by the seemingly never-ending influx of foreigners, Gavin Rae of Dundee has shown the way for the home brigade. The young midfielder must have feared for his future when Ivano Bonetti was appointed manager and started bringing in players from all round Europe and South America. But Rae defied the odds to make his place in the team secure and capped off a wonderful season by playing from the start of Scotland's 1–1 draw against Poland in March. That honour made him the first Dundee player to represent Scotland since Robert Connor, 15 years earlier.

Needless to say, the Aberdonian's stunning form for the Dark Blues attracted the attention of bigger outfits, but boss Bonetti warned that he would not leave Dens Park on the cheap. English Premiership sides Chelsea and Ipswich were both credited with an interest in the youngster, but the Dark Blues' chief was insistant about Rae's value.

'I'm not surprised that clubs are interested in him,' he said at the time, 'but he is going nowhere. He is a very important player for Dundee. He is

Dundee United's Charlie Miller uses his strength to hold off Celtic midfielder Neil Lennon

good enough to play in Serie A, and, being realistic, I know that offers are bound to come in for him. But I also know that the longer he stays at Dens, the more valuable he will become.'

Perhaps the best of many top-class performances was his starring show in Dundee's 2–0 win at Ibrox in February, when, along with Giorgi Nemsadze, he ran the show. It was a night that saw manager Ivano Bonetti label Gavin as 'worth £10 million'.

Rae, though, appreciates the help he has had from his multi-national team-mates.

'Playing beside the likes of Claudio Caniggia,' he said, 'was tremendous. There is so much to learn from him. For a man of his age, his attitude and work-rate is phenomenal.'

Now Caniggia is, of course, plying his trade at Ibrox, but Rae has already proved himself more than ready to take over the mantle as the top star at Dens Park.

CHARLIE MILLER DUNDEE UNITED

Charlie Miller could be described as a number of things – talented, gifted even – or, if you were being less charitable, wasteful and naive. But few people in the Scottish game would have begrudged him his re-emergence from the wilderness last season as he dragged Dundee United away from the relegation trapdoor that had seemed for so long to be their fate.

The recovery of the Tannadice side after an appalling start to the campaign synchronised perfectly with the recovery of Miller's career. The boy who had appeared to have the world at his feet as he broke through to the Rangers' first team had shot himself in those self-same feet with a lack of application and discipline that eventually forced Dick Advocaat to terminate his stay at Ibrox.

That jolt should have been sufficient to get

Miller back on to the straight and narrow, but instead he wandered aimlessly with English clubs like Watford, which, if truth be told, were not deserving of his immense talent. That he could not even get a game for the Vicarage Road side underlined just how low his stock had fallen. But Dundee United manager Alex Smith remembered how much ability was being thrown away. And the man who had taken over an ailing Tannadice side after the departure of Paul Sturrock only two games into the League season believed Miller could be as good for United as they could be for him.

So it proved. As the fitness returned, so did the commanding form that saw Miller dominate countless games after the winter break. In fact, his performances were of such a high and consistent standard that he even won his first cap, albeit about five years after he should have done. And the chances are, when he played against Poland in April, no one was prouder than his Tannadice boss – and with good reason. In the game, as in his life, Miller showed a new maturity. And this now allows him to reflect on mistakes made.

KEIGAN PARKER ST JOHNSTONE

Keigan Parker is a young man going places – but St Johnstone fans hope not for quite some time as they recognise he is the jewel in their crown. The McDiarmid Park crowd were starved of any real success last season as their club's decent start turned into a stuttering middle and disappointing end. Mirroring that slip in fortune was the performance level of young striker Parker. For much of the campaign he was running neck and neck with eventual winner, Celtic's Stilian Petrov, in the race to be named Scotland's Young Player of the Year.

Goals came as easily as plaudits to the hot-shot, and he looked to be on course to fire St Johnstone to a top-six finish at least, with qualifying for Europe not out of the question. Unfortunately, Parker went off the boil along with the Saints' performances. Goals and points dried up, a combination that is guaranteed not only to frustrate but also to bring the bottom half of the table ever closer.

But it should not have come as any surprise that the Parker route to the top should have one or two potholes to negotiate on the way. Like any

young player, he will be susceptible to dips in form. And, just as surely, he will blast back in exciting fashion to have people drooling over his ability once again. The man who gave him his first-team chance at just 17 years of age, St Johnstone manager Sandy Clark, is a founder member of the Parker fan club. And, as a former striker himself, Clark recognises the importance of experience and support in the position, which is why he is keen to follow the example of a manager who knows a thing or two about nurturing young talent.

'If you listen to Sir Alex Ferguson,' Clark explained, 'he will tell you that you have got to be careful and protect them. You can play kids at any age, as long as they are good enough. But they must be ready, physically and mentally, to cope.'

Cope Parker most certainly will. And everyone at McDiarmid Park is keeping their fingers crossed that this popular young man will go on to realise the potential they all know he carries, preferably in the blue of Saints.

Keigan Parker – the jewel in St Johnstone's crown

Greg Strong,
the defender who won
Henrik Larsson's respect

GREG STRONG MOTHERWELL

Greg Strong didn't win any medals last season with Motherwell, but he did win the respect of Scotland's top striker, Henrik Larsson. While the Celtic hit-man was firing his way to a record 53 goals for the season, Fir Park defender Strong was spiking his guns every time they met. In fact, neither Larsson nor his striking partner, Chris Sutton, managed to get the ball past Strong and into the Motherwell net. And that's a record of which the Strong-man, who arrived from Bolton near the end of season 1999–2000, is proud to boast.

'At the end of last season,' the uncompromising Englishman said, 'some newspapers carried pictures of every goal Henrik had scored. The lads in our dressing room noticed we did not feature in any of them. I think a few defenders would be proud to be able to say that.'

But Strong makes no secret of Motherwell's success against Larsson and company. It's all down to hard work.

'Our tactics,' he explained, 'were always just to shut the Celtic players down as much as possible to prevent chances being created. It seemed to work for the most part last season, when I felt we defended against them quite well in open play. Unfortunately, we let ourselves down a few times when defending set pieces, and that's where we conceded most of our goals against them.'

Sutton had another reason to regret coming up against his countryman, as the Celtic striker was sent off in only his second game for Celtic when he clashed with Strong in their game at Parkhead.

But there is more to Strong's game than sheer power, and he hopes to show that this season. He also hopes that Motherwell are not involved in the dogfight at the bottom of the division but recognises that experienced players like him will have to be ready to do their bit and that Lady Luck will also have to be a bit kinder.

'At the start of last season,' Strong said, 'it was very difficult for us because of the amount of players we had out injured. At one point we were without as many as eight men who would probably be in the starting line-up, and I think any team would find it difficult in those circumstances.'

ANDY McLAREN KILMARNOCK

When Kilmarnock manager Bobby Williamson announced to the world that he had taken Andy McLaren under his wing at Rugby Park, there were those who suggested the former Rangers' striker must have headed one ball too many during his playing career. McLaren was, after all, known across the length and breadth of Britain not so much for his ability to weave through defences but for his inability to find a path that avoided the temptations of drink and drugs. The man who started off as a starlet at Dundee United had headed South to conquer England in a £100,000 move to Reading, but the bottle got the better of him, and soon 'hitting the bar' had a deeper and more sinister meaning.

To be fair to the man, he faced up to his problem. He had to, when the English FA banned

Kilmarnock's Andy McLaren celebrates

him after he had fallen foul of a random dope test. But even with the will to kick the habit, there are not many vacancies for footballers with an alcohol problem in their kit bag. It was only when Williamson opened the door to McLaren and he started a three-month trial at Rugby Park that his career began to recover. So quickly, in fact, that he was voted Player of the Month in Scotland for August and also found himself offered a new, permanent contract. Indeed, so well did he repay his manager's faith in him that Scotland boss Craig Brown found it impossible to ignore his skills. And McLaren's fairytale was completed when he won his first Scotland cap against Poland in April. For the 27-year-old who had been to hell and back, the shabby stadium in Bydgoszcz must have seemed like the promised land.

But it was not a cap awarded out of sympathy. McLaren's outstanding performances for Killie ensured it was his by right. Ironically, he was in the company of an Alcoholics Anonymous counsellor when the call came that allowed him to say, 'My name is Andy McLaren. I'm a Scotland player.' McLaren had been linked with a Scotland call-up earlier in the season, but this time it was for real, even if it came at the 11th hour after Brown's

Colin Cameron played so well he earned himself a move to Wolves

squad had suffered its normal batch of withdrawals.

'The call came out of the blue,' McLaren explained at the time. 'I phoned my mum right away, and that was quite emotional. It is like that for my whole family because they have been through it all with me. They have known the hard times. This time last year I wasn't long out of the clinic. To get back to any level would have been an achievement, but this is dream stuff. It is still hard to take in, but a lot of good people have helped me along the way.'

None more so than Williamson, who had faith when, at best, others had only pity.

'I am grateful to Killie for giving me the chance to get back into the game,' McLaren said. 'I've really enjoyed the last few months, and the dressing room at Killie has been terrific.'

And McLaren has already said thanks in the best possible way, by helping the Rugby Park side reach the CIS League Cup final before finishing fourth in the SPL and qualifying for Europe.

COLIN CAMERON HEARTS

Hearts re-emergence as a major player in the struggle to break the Old Firm's stranglehold in Scotland got back on track last season as the influence of new manager Craig Levein began to kick in. While the former Tynecastle defender worked hard off the pitch to put his theories across to his new charges, the job of ensuring the game plan was put into action on the field was left in the more than capable hands of captain Colin Cameron.

The pocket dynamo – who first came to prominence as a member of the First Division Raith Rovers side that caused a major upset by beating Celtic in the Coca-Cola Cup final in 1994 – can always be guaranteed to lead by example. And his driving influence saw Hearts recover from a dodgy start to the season and move into a strong challenging position for Europe.

Cameron and company were spurred on by the memory of how they were knocked out of the UEFA Cup by Stuttgart. That first-round tie saw the German side reduced to nine men in the second leg at Tynecastle, but they clung on as Hearts won 3–2, a result good enough to put Stuttgart through on away goals.

Cameron was as sick as his team-mates, but he bounced back from that disappointment to pick up form and points so impressively that not only did Hearts start to climb the table but Cameron found himself adding to his cap collection. The highlight of his international year was scoring against San Marino in the World Cup qualifier at Hampden. Unfortunately, that achievement was all but buried under the avalanche of condemnation that followed Colin Hendry's infamous use of an elbow during the game.

Cameron shrugged off being robbed of his moment of glory and went back to doing what he does best, playing his heart out for Hearts. The battle with Kilmarnock for a UEFA Cup place had still to be settled, and Cameron showed his determination when he said, 'At the start of the season, Europe was always our aim. We perceive ourselves to be the third biggest club in the country. And, if that's the case, with four places up for grabs this year, we certainly should be qualifying for Europe every other season.'

They lost out on the final day when Kilmarnock pulled off a shock home win over a less than full strength Celtic side who had one eye on the Scottish Cup final a week later. But that has just added more fuel to Cameron's fired-up ambition to get back to challenging for trophies and the European places that go with them.

IAN FERGUSON DUNFERMLINE

It must have taken all of Dunfermline manager Jimmy Calderwood's powers of persuasion to tempt Ian Ferguson to East End Park as the Pars chased promotion to the Premier League. It was a major wrench for Fergie, one of the shining lights of Rangers' nine-in-a-row team, to leave Ibrox in January 2000, after 12 years as a True Blue.

During that glory spell he won every honour in the Scottish game along with nine international caps. But the powerhouse midfield man wanted to prove he could still play at the top level. And, according to his delighted manager, he has succeeded big time. Calderwood said, 'Ian hates losing – in fact, I don't think I've come across a player in my whole career who hates losing more.'

After helping the Pars to promotion, his sterling performances last season helped them to

Ian Ferguson proved a superb buy for Dunfermline

within a whisker of a top-six finish, losing out only on goal difference to Dundee on the last day before the split. His dominant play has made him very much a fans' favourite, much as he has been throughout a career that has seen him ply his trade at Clyde and St Mirren as well as Rangers. His commitment to Dunfermline is now total, but his Ibrox days will always be with him, as witnessed by the treatment he receives from Celtic fans in particular. It is, in a peculiar way, something of a backhanded compliment, as they are simply acknowledging the damage he inflicted on their favourites over the years.

Fergie is now at the ripe old age of 34, but he is still a class act. He did, in fact, have the chance to move towards the end of last season when Rangers' Australian feeder club, Northern Spirit, tried to tempt him to Sydney. But not even the thought of life in the stunning Southern Hemisphere city could tempt him from his Scottish roots, and he returned from Down Under refreshed and ready to go again.

One thing is for sure and that is that anyone who lines up against Fergie this season will know they have been in a game.

DAVID BINGHAM LIVINGSTON

The Bingo caller was asked to work overtime at Livingston's games as they shot towards last season's First Division championship. But the reward is a full house virtually every week now as the SPL's new boys enjoy life in the top division.

Of course, the Bingo in question is Livvy hot-shot, David Bingham, whose name seemed to be forever on the lips of the announcer at Almondvale

David Bingham's guile and determination played an integral part in Livingston's promotion as he banged in the goals that propelled Jim Leishman's side to promotion. The Livvy fans never tired of cheering the exploits of the former Dunfermline striker, whose work-rate and willingness to shoot on sight have made him a real asset throughout his career. But no matter the success he has enjoyed up until now, there is no doubting that last season was the most productive Bingham has ever enjoyed. So much so, he was the runaway winner of the First Division Player of the Year award. He had previously won the Third Division award with Forfar and added the Second Division prize after his first year with Livvy. How he would love to battle Henrik Larsson and company to make it the full set this season.

The real satisfaction last term came from knowing that he had helped put Livingston on the football map, including a Scottish Cup run that took them all the way to a semi-final at Hampden. Unfortunately for Bingham and his team-mates, waiting for them there was Alex McLeish's excellent Hibs side, who ran out 3–0 winners. But that proved to be one of the few setbacks in a season Bingham will look back on with pride.

Jim Leishman has been a long-time admirer of his striker's abilities, and their Dunfermline background gives them many shared memories. But it is the future that interests them most and, together, Bingham and Leishman believe they can make an impact on the top division. Bingham is not the biggest striker in the land, but what he lacks in height he more than makes up for in guile and determination. These are attributes all Livvy fans will hope to see again throughout this testing campaign, and the chances are there will be more than two fat ladies cheering on Bingo.

PHILIP MCGUIRE ABERDEEN

Philip McGuire has a big responsibility on his young shoulders. Only just out of his teens, the central defender is one of the bright young talents Aberdeen are banking on to help them return to the glory days that saw them lift championships, cups and European trophies. That might seem like light years away from the troubled times the club has endured of late. But, even through this dark passage, there have been shining lights to keep hope burning brightly for the Pittodrie fans.

One of them is undoubtedly McGuire, whose progress last season marked him down as one to

Philip McGuire is a shining light at Pittodrie

watch. Much to the youngster's annoyance, he made more headlines for an act of folly than a moment of brilliance. At Ibrox in February he decided to try his hand at peace-making as Rangers' Tugay and Dons' skipper Derek Whyte got entangled. The upshot was a red card for Glasgow-born McGuire – one of two he collected in the season along with a handful of yellows – and a lesson learned. 'I went about it the wrong way,' he recalled, 'because I shouldn't have pushed Tugay. Instead, I should have put my arms around my own player and dragged him away.'

Perhaps the automatic reaction to rush to the rescue of a team-mate stems from the one-for-all culture McGuire has been brought up in during his formative years at Pittodrie. 'The way we were coached in the youth team,' he explained, 'we were always told to stick up for one another. We were always battlers, and I think that has shown as we have come through into the first team.'

McGuire doesn't mean that in a fisticuffs way but more in the manner in which the young Dons side has battled to repay the faith that manager Ebbe Skovdahl has invested in them. Even when things were not going well for McGuire and his team-mates last term, the boss stuck by them. The reward for this should begin to arrive this season, if the talent that undoubtedly lies within the side can begin to blossom. Skovdahl can at least rest easy that in McGuire he has a young man of some substance.

He made his debut in season 1999–2000, a game he is unlikely ever to forget as it was won by Celtic to the tune of 6–0. Rather than dwell on his horrendous start, however, McGuire has put it down to part of the steep learning curve he is prepared to endure to become a better player. And Aberdeen fans will confirm he is definitely getting there.

CELTIC KEEP THE PRESSURE ON

MARTIN O'NEILL is carving a niche for himself in the folklore of Celtic after taking the club to within touching distance of their first treble since the days of Jock Stein. The latest instalment of the fairy story that is his first season in charge of the club saw Didier Agathe – a £35,000 'hunch' purchase – score the only goal of the game at Pittodrie to leave Celtic requiring just six more points to secure the championship.

The victory all but brought O'Neill to the point of conceding this is a side that can go all the way. Up until now he has steadfastly refused to allow the inhabitants of the hencoop to be counted. But even the Celtic manager finally accepts it all adds up to a gloriously successful campaign.

It was refreshing to see O'Neill drop the 'if we win it, not when we win it' front and talk openly about clinching the title with just two more victories. Victory over Dundee on Wednesday and St Mirren on Saturday will see Celtic crowned champions – and they will be worthy champions.

The proud manager summed it up perfectly when he said, 'We have scored 20-odd goals more than anyone else and we have been the outstandingly consistent team in the League. Our record proves that.'

That's why, at 2.40 next Saturday afternoon, O'Neill will rush out on to the park and celebrate with every one of his players. He will know it is results like the one achieved against Aberdeen last night that will have carried them to victory. Pretty it may not have been, rich with goals it certainly was not. But it was another three vital steps towards the finishing-line and that's all that matters at this stage of the title race. It was even appropriate that Didier Agathe should be the man to score the all-important goal after 73 minutes of what had been an evenly-contested affair as, with this one kick, suddenly the sum of his contribution far outweighed its content.

The man who was snatched from the bargain-basement earlier in the season looked anything but a £35,000 player. Joos Valgaeren's throw-in on the left was headed on by Alan Thompson and then Henrik Larsson. The ball fell to Lubo Moravcik but cannoned off David Rowson's shin, falling perfectly for Agathe who was hovering around the penalty spot. His speed of thought matched his speed of foot and he swivelled on the spot before firing a low shot through the legs of the unsuspecting Jamie McAllister and past an unsighted Ryan Esson in the Dons goal.

For all their effort, Aberdeen never posed much of a threat to Rab Douglas's goal. Their best chance had fallen to the useful Darren Mackie in 62 minutes when he outstripped Valgaeren – no mean feat – and fired in a shot that clipped the far post. Ultimately, however, the spurned chances had no bearing on the result, and the impressive Celtic travelling support were happy enough as they entertained their Dons counterparts with their repertoire of championship songs. Chances are they will get another airing on Wednesday before Saturday's main performance. Certainly, old Bhoy Derek Whyte reckons they will have plenty to sing about. He believes their Celtic heroes have taken over Rangers' mantle in more ways than one.

'They are doing exactly what Rangers have been doing for years,' the Aberdeen defender said. 'Grinding out results.'

CELTIC
TOUGH IT OUT

CELTIC came in from the cold at Tynecastle last night to send a clear message to title challengers Rangers – we are not feeling the heat.

The Ibrox side had hoped that their 2–0 victory over Dunfermline on Saturday would not only take them to within six points of the League leaders, but would also uncover a fatal flaw in Celtic's make-up. To be fair, all the ingredients for a recipe for disaster were in place. Celtic had played only a relatively easy Scottish Cup tie – the 4–1 third-round win at Stranraer – since 2 January. The wintry conditions at Tynecastle were not suited to their quick-passing game. And they lost defensive rock Joos Valgaeren after only five minutes of frantic play.

However, rather than crack under the pressure, this Celtic side proved once and for all they are the real deal. Of course, it helped enormously that, by the time the unfortunate Valgaeren was landing badly on his left ankle, Henrik Larsson had already put them one goal ahead. A second goal in 67 minutes sealed the points but, as the Hearts fans deserted, the Celtic fans demanded. Only a hat-trick from their super hero would satisfy them, and it duly arrived with eight minutes remaining.

It was a hard-fought match with both sides committed to giving their all. In Hearts' case, for no reward. But their midfield general, Colin Cameron, reckons they were chasing a lost cause from the opening minutes when they committed the cardinal sin.

'The one thing you don't want to do against Celtic or Rangers is to lose an early goal,' he explained. 'When you have to push forward for 87 minutes with the type of players Celtic have, they will finish you off.

'But 3–0 is not a fair score-line. At 1–0 we had a chance from a free kick that was nearly turned in for an own goal. As it was, we only got a corner, and from there they won the ball and went up the park to score their second.

'That basically killed it. We had been pushing for the equaliser, but that meant we left spaces in behind, which guys like Henrik Larsson and Neil Lennon will always exploit. So, it was disappointing to lose, but you can see they are a quality side.'

Indeed you can, and the credit for that must go to manager O'Neill, who started the game with all seven of the signings he has made since his arrival in the summer. While continuing to insist that they are not anywhere near the finished article, he is delighted with the effort and football the team continues to produce. Now they can add bottle to their CV and O'Neill heaped on the praise.

'The attitude of the players is second to none,' he insisted. 'They keep going and play some nice stuff. I knew that, regardless of what had happened in previous matches, this was going to be a really difficult 90 minutes with Hearts really wound up for it and us not having played in midweek. All of those things were a bit of a concern, and at 1–0 they were always in the game with a chance. So I was pleased to see the second goal go in. You can draw a bit of confidence from that, and a bit of relief. Overall, our performance merited the win.'

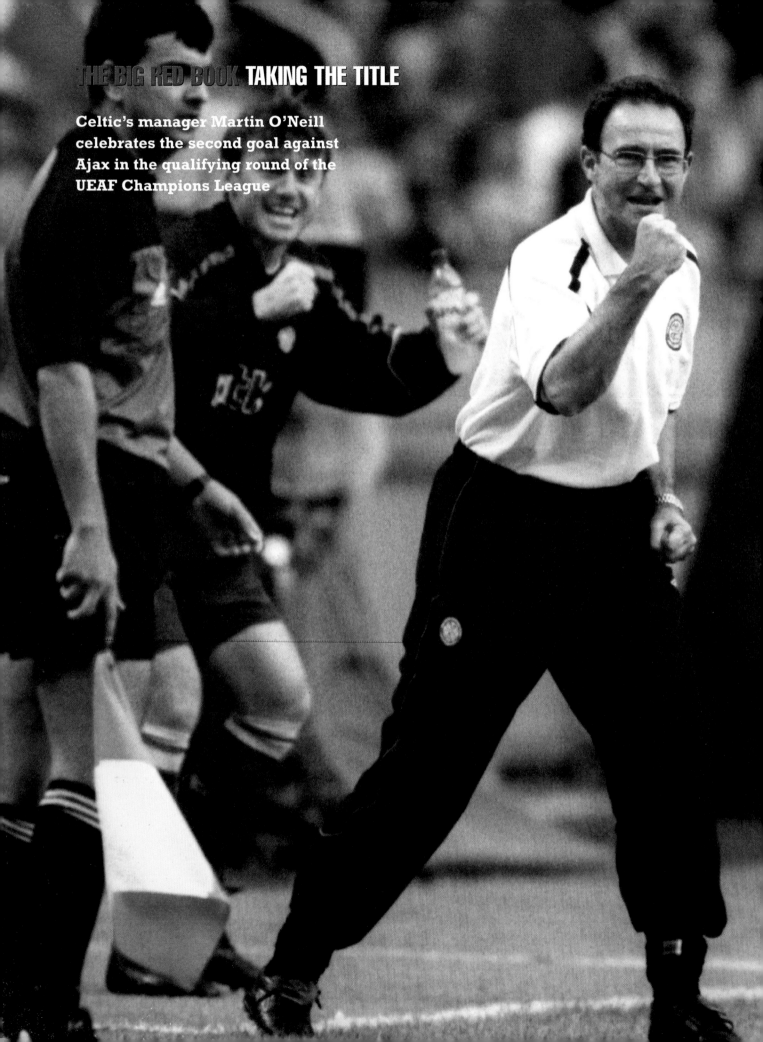

Celtic's manager Martin O'Neill celebrates the second goal against Ajax in the qualifying round of the UEAF Champions League

MARTIN O'NEILL

Martin O'Neill stepped outside Celtic Park and addressed the throng of Hoops' fans waiting to welcome the new manager. That day in June last year he knew enough about the history of the club to ensure that his first words to the supporters would not sound hollow or act as a millstone around his neck. But O'Neill also realised that the beleaguered fans needed some hope, something to cling to as the new season approached. Above all, they needed a reason to believe there would be no repeat of the disastrous season endured under the leadership of John Barnes and Kenny Dalglish.

So it was that O'Neill told the Celtic supporters who turned out to greet him, 'I will do everything in my power to bring success back to this club.' It was succinct. It became a prophecy. Eleven months later, the goods were delivered with the club's first treble for 32 years secured. However, not even O'Neill could have predicted that his first year in the manager's seat would prove to be so productive. He admits that he would have been satisfied with closing the 21-point gap on Rangers,

> **'I will do everything in my power to bring success back to this club'**

a margin of victory the Ibrox club had enjoyed in their romp to the championship the year before.

But, from a long way out, it was clear that Celtic were going to prove uncatchable in their race for the title, clinching it as early as Grand National day, 7 April. By then, O'Neill had already got the club off to a flying start by winning the CIS League Cup, his first trophy as Celtic manager. And, of course, the Scottish Cup was to follow to complete the Grand Slam for the club and guarantee a place in Celtic folklore for O'Neill.

He is the 13th manager in the club's history, but not one of his 12 predecessors was taken to the hearts of the supporters as quickly as the Ulsterman. And that is a relief to the man who studied Law before embarking on a successful career as a footballer. He knew the jury would be out on him until he presented a winning case. Now, any fears he harboured about stepping up from the comfort of the manager's office at Leicester to the hot seat in Glasgow's East End have long been banished from his mind. The chance to manage Celtic had been a long-held dream. But, like most

A pat on the back for Cup final hero Didier Agathe, one of the seven players O'Neill brought to the club in his first season

of us, when it comes to turning dreams into reality, a little trepidation tends to accompany opportunity.

However, there was never going to be anything frightening enough to stop O'Neill embracing the job. His father, Leo, had once told him back in their home town of Kilrea that anyone should walk to Parkhead to accept the manager's position if it was offered to them. These words were not lost on O'Neill when the call came to lead Celtic from the wilderness. He had developed

deep roots at Filbert Street, but the pull to branch out proved too strong to deny. That's why, when it eventually came to decision time, O'Neill reveals it took all of two and a half seconds for him to say 'I do'. At that moment, a marriage made in paradise, if not heaven, was confirmed.

And, astonishing though the job he did at Filbert Street was – leading them to the top half of the Premiership and to Worthington Cup success with the bonus of Europe that came with it – that was to prove as nothing compared to the resurrection he has overseen at Celtic Park. He has taken a decaying institution and transformed it into a club that can once more hold its head high.

The poor results achieved by John Barnes and his mentor, Kenny Dalglish, are but bitter memories to Celtic fans, who must still be pinching themselves, desperately hoping they can truly believe the events of season 2000–1. Today, with the three domestic trophies sparkling in front of the players in the official team line-up photos, they can believe – truly believe. And while Henrik Larsson's 53 goals, Neil Lennon's driving in midfield and Johan Mjallby's outstanding form in defence were all major contributions to this success, the fans know the man they have to thank above all others for restoring their pride is Martin O'Neill.

In less time than even he imagined possible, he has delivered. Unassuming and self-effacing he may be, but behind the look of bemusement and bewilderment that he likes to present lies a shrewd thinker. He knows how to get the best out of a situation and, more importantly, the best out of the players at his disposal. Players who had been performing well suddenly performed better. Others who had not shown anything under previous managers were gradually converted into heroes.

O'Neill proved he can also spot a player, bring him into the side and quickly reap a reward. Seven players were brought to the club in his first season – Chris Sutton, Joos Valgaeren, Alan Thompson, Didier Agathe, Rab Douglas, Neil Lennon and finally Ramon Vega. Every one played a major part in the club's success, an unprecedented return for the £13m net expenditure the club's board had had to approve. The last incumbent of the Celtic Park manager's office to have such an eye for a 'Celtic' player was the late, great Jock Stein. In O'Neill's eyes, however, any comparison with the man who led Celtic to European Cup glory and nine championships in a row are as spurious as they are unwelcome.

'Listen,' he said, clearly embarrassed, 'I have got a million, million miles to go before you can ever even say I am in the shadow of Jock Stein.'

He is wise enough to settle for following in the Big Man's footsteps without ever claiming to be the

> **'I have got a million, million miles to go before you can ever even say I am in the shadow of Jock Stein'**

one to fill his shoes. Stein may have been the last Celtic manager to be able to pose in front of the three Scottish trophies, but O'Neill knows he is only standing at the beginning of the road to the kind of sustained glory that Stein brought to the club. For now, he is happy to have taken the first step and delighted that the heart-wrenching decision he had to make last summer has proved to be so right. He had previously been accused of vertigo after he turned down the opportunity to manage what many regarded as top-flight club Leeds. But Celtic? Well, that was a different proposition altogether.

Mind you, O'Neill still finds time to let a smile cross his lips as he reads accounts of how other managers lay claim to virtually making the decision for him. And he scoffs at reports that he is here on the advice of Leeds' boss David O'Leary and former Hoops manager Lou Macari.

'I remember well the conversations I had with both David and Lou,' said O'Neill, 'and they didn't go along the lines of what I've been reading. Apparently, David has claimed to have spoken to me before I came to Celtic, telling me I'd be a coward if I didn't take the job. The truth is, the first time I met him was in Brussels during the Euro 2000 finals, by which time I was in place as the Celtic manager. His reaction was to tell me I'd taken on an extremely tough job simply because, in his opinion, Rangers were miles ahead of us at that time. It's the same situation with Lou, who, funnily enough, actually told me I'd be mad to leave Leicester. The honest truth is, once the club contacted me, there were only three people who I bothered to consult – my wife and two daughters. Once I had their thumbs-up, not accepting the offer to come here was never an option to me.'

Not even the fact that he was regarded as an also-ran in the race for the position behind long-time favourite Guus Hiddink could cause O'Neill any anxious moments.

'I don't care if I was the first or the hundredth choice,' he explained. 'It's what you do with the job that's important.'

And O'Neill knew before he set foot inside Celtic Park what a big job it was, one he could not hope to tackle without the support of some trusted friends and colleagues.

'It was simply a case of getting started,' he recalled, 'and recruiting my two cohorts, John Robertson and Steve Walford.'

These are the men who know him better than anybody, and acknowledging the contribution of his right-hand men comes naturally to O'Neill. Now he hopes the three of them will continue to have reasons to be glad they decided to make the move North. Naturally cautious, O'Neill likes nothing better than to say that, if results start to go against Celtic, they will all be shown the door.

'I know if we don't retain the championship, I won't be here, but that's the nature of the game,' he insists.

With the groundwork done, however, the likelihood of him being asked to vacate the seat seems as remote as Celtic playing in blue. As O'Neill said, 'The stadium is in place, the support is here. Now it's up to me to get the team.' On the evidence of last season, that's a job well in hand.

Paul Lambert and Tom Boyd with the Scottish Cup

Happy bhoys as the League title is won

Martin O'Neill holds the Scottish Cup aloft

Alex Ferguson
with his mentor
Jock Stein

SIR ALEX FERGUSON GOVAN'S GUVNOR

ALEX Ferguson will welcome Celtic to Old Trafford tonight with an effusive smile. Then he will become grumpy.

For the most part this Knight of the Realm is one of the kindest, friendliest and most charismatic of men you could ever wish to meet. But once the chewing gum is placed between his lips, once the business gets serious – as it will when he steps from the tunnel to guide his Manchester United side against Celtic in the testimonial for Ryan Giggs – there will be a metamorphosis and Ferguson will don an impregnable cloak of competitiveness.

This inner desire, a fascination for the battlefield, is a far cry from the other side of his character that will see him take 12 or 24 hours out of a gruelling schedule to promote charitable causes throughout the land. And when any project featuring his birthplace in Govan comes calling, wild horses would be required to drag him away from fulfilling the appointment.

Within that working-class background, where he felt a sense of injustice poured down upon those around him, the seeds of his great success can probably be identified. While others succumbed, Ferguson's sense of social justice prevailed. Allied to a native wit garnered on the streets of the south side of Glasgow, a superb intelligence and a body clock minus an alarm, the package was as formidable as you could find. Ultimately, it has provided an incredible array of trophies.

Along the way Ferguson may well be entitled to be called the greatest manager in the history of British football, but he would forcibly dispute that point. He has two heroes in his life, his father and Jock Stein.

'When I was a boy I used to look out the window trying to spot my father coming home from work,' he said. 'It was near impossible because all you could see was a sea of bunnets going along the road. There are no bunnets left, little work, and that is a tragedy.'

By the time he joined up with big Jock in the mid-'80s, Ferguson was already a successful manager in his own right. His Aberdeen team arrived in Glasgow with a purpose, and his players of the time – the likes of Alex McLeish, Willie Miller and Mark McGhee – tell tales of dressing-room team-talks at Ibrox and Parkhead that would not have been out of place in the trenches during the First World War.

The titles and trophies rolled in, alongside the European Cup-Winners' Cup, collected on a memorable night in Gothenburg in 1983 courtesy of a 2–1 victory over the world's most famous club, Real Madrid.

He could have moved to Rangers but was disgusted when a newspaper revealed there could be a question mark over his credentials because his wife is Catholic. That is not a topic up for discussion nowadays. Indeed, it was never spoken of in public. But of all the factors within football that have driven him to his current pre-eminent status, there can be no doubt the time he spent with Stein was the fulcrum. They were the sorcerer and his apprentice. The magician had already witnessed the qualities required for succession to the state-of-the-art talents he had delivered at Celtic during the 1960s. The lad, comparatively anyway, was always ready to learn because that had been a fundamental of his life.

Stein's untimely death left Ferguson devastated. 'As painful as losing my father,' he said, but he was left to combine his job at Aberdeen with the unenviable task of taking Scotland to the World Cup Finals in Mexico in 1986.

The resilience he has shown at Old Trafford since the autumn of 1986 has been a testament to the character forged in Govan and enhanced through his years with Aberdeen and his alliance with Stein. He took a European Cup to Manchester in 1999, a Cup-Winners' Cup in 1991, and seven Premiership championships from a possible nine. Tonight, when Celtic enter one of the greatest arenas in world football, they can be sure of applause from every corner of the ground. But watch out for the man chewing the gum. He doesn't play friendlies.

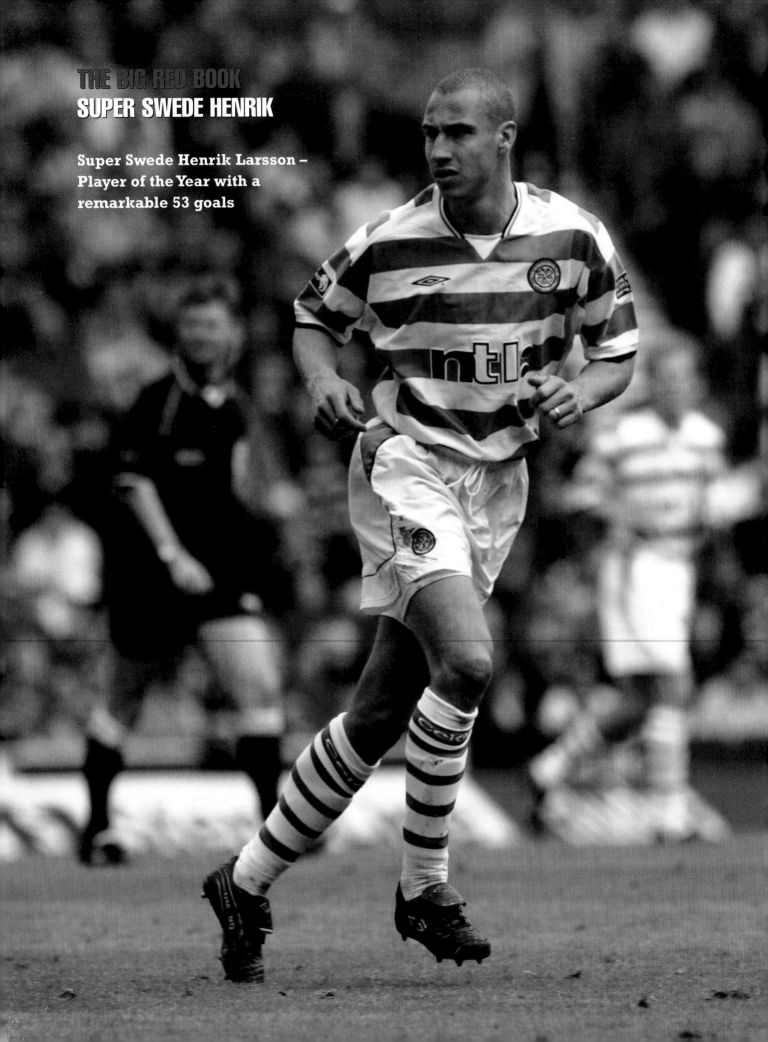

SUPER SWEDE HENRIK

Super Swede Henrik Larsson –
Player of the Year with a
remarkable 53 goals

SUPER SWEDE HENRIK

The Monopolies Commission should take a serious look at Henrik Larsson. The Celtic striker wanted it all last season – and very nearly got it. As if winner's medals from the Bank of Scotland SPL, the CIS Insurance League Cup and the Tennent's Scottish Cup were not enough to satisfy him, the Super Swede also made a clean sweep of the individual honours' lists.

The Player of the Year accolades awarded by both the Scottish Football Writers and the Scottish Professional Footballers have his name deservedly engraved upon them after he lit up the headlines with a remarkable 53 goals in the campaign. That tally saw him shatter Charlie Nicholas' 18-year-old record for goals scored by a Celt in any season since the war, and the 35 League goals that formed the centrepiece of his hit list were good enough to give him the Golden Shoe as the top striker in Europe.

This collection of trophies alone would be something to look back upon with pride, but, more importantly, Larsson emerged from the season of his life with a new contract that will keep him in the Hoops until the summer of 2004. His decision to

Everyone waited with bated breath to see if the Henrik of old could re-emerge. And they didn't have to keep their fingers crossed for long

further commit himself to Celtic put the ideal seal on the perfect season, which had more highlights than Frank McAvennie's hair yet had started with a serious question mark hanging over the Swede.

He had managed to make an appearance as a substitute in the final game of the previous season as he carefully eased himself back into action after recovering from the leg break he suffered against Lyon in November 1999. The odd flicker of genius during Sweden's bid for glory at Euro 2000 confirmed that he was on course to pick up the reins as the King of Kings in the Celtic side when season 2000–1 began under the watchful eye of new manager Martin O'Neill. Everyone waited with bated breath to see if the Henrik of old could re-emerge. And they didn't have to keep their fingers crossed for long, as Larsson got on the scoresheet in the opening fixture at Tannadice.

His new striking partner, £6m buy Chris Sutton, was also on the mark that day to secure the points with a 2–1 win, and a partnership that was to bear fruit throughout the season had shown the first sign of blossoming. Sutton describes Larsson as 'priceless' and 'the best I

Henrik Larsson in action against St Mirren

have ever played with'. The respect is reciprocated, with Larsson acknowledging the massive contribution the Englishman made to his goal-laden season.

The effectiveness of the most lethal partnership to hit Scottish football for decades was best illustrated in the final game before the winter break. Kilmarnock had travelled to Celtic Park full of hope that they could maintain their challenge for a European place. They left wondering what had hit them as they reflected on a 6–0 thrashing that saw Sutton net twice and Larsson score four.

The pair also hit the headlines when Kilmarnock provided the opposition in the CIS League Cup final in March. But, this time, the fortunes of the strikers could hardly have been more polarised. While Larsson hit a match-winning hat-trick, Sutton hit Gary Holt with a tackle deemed bad enough to merit a red card. Leading 1–0 with a numerical disadvantage for the final 30 minutes of a major Cup final might bring out the

Larsson's talent is matched only by his modesty

defensive side in most players – but not Larsson. He took advantage of the extra space to score two more, the second of which he later described as his best goal of the season. He picked the ball up on the halfway line, ran through the Kilmarnock defence and side-stepped Gordon Marshall in the Killie goal before coolly flicking the ball over the line – alchemy by any other name.

But Larsson's talent is matched only by his modesty, and he quickly attempted to turn the spotlight on his team-mates.

'That just shows the character this team has,' he said. 'We never give up. We were 1–0 up when Chris was sent off, so that made it a bit easier. But we fought for each other, and nobody wanted to give up. That's why we won 3–0.'

'I was in the stand last year,' he continued, 'and watched the final from there, so I was pleased to have the chance to play this time.'

And play he did. In fact, this was one of four appearances he made at Hampden in the course

Celtic strike pair Chris Sutton and Henrik Larsson proved more than a handful for Scottish defences

of the season – and he made the national stadium's nets bulge no fewer than nine times.

Prior to the aforementioned treble against Killie, he hit a double in the tousy CIS League Cup semi-final win over Rangers. The Scottish Cup was to prove just as productive, with two goals in the semi-final victory over Dundee United, and a double in the final itself against Hibs was to be the crowning glory in King Henrik's golden year.

Another undoubted high point was notching his 50th goal of the campaign in the 3–0 defeat of Rangers at Ibrox in April. Larsson admitted that that strike, from the most acute of angles, had special significance and revealed, 'That goal is one that will live with me forever. It doesn't get a lot better than the feeling I had at the final whistle at Ibrox. To score my 50th goal of the season, and beat Rangers 3–0 at their own ground, is an amazing feeling.'

> **'That goal is one that will live with me forever. It doesn't get a lot better than the feeling I had at the final whistle at Ibrox'**

Of course, news of Larsson's propensity for putting the ball into the net travelled far and wide, bringing unwanted attention from clubs in England and farther afield. While many Celtic fans – not to mention Martin O'Neill – must have lost sleep over the prospect of their star striker being enticed to ply his trade elsewhere, Larsson continued to knock in the goals, content in the knowledge that his only ambition is to continue to enjoy his family life here in Scotland for another three years before returning to his homeland, where he has already set himself his next challenge.

In a rare moment, when the guard he adopts to protect the privacy of his home life was allowed to drop, Larsson admitted one of the few ambitions he still has to fulfil is to return home to Sweden when his career with Celtic is over and turn out for the little home-town club where it all began for him.

Larsson in control in the Scottish Cup Final

Henrik Larsson bursts clear of the Dundee defence

'I might go back and play with my first club, Hogaborg BK,' he explained. 'By then I'll have been away for more than ten years, so I'm just going to have a look and see what I want to do. Hopefully, the body is feeling right and my health and everything is good.'

The only doubt is that Larsson will ever feel any better than he does today. He has returned from injury better than before, and even the presence of a steel rod running the length of his shinbone failed to prevent him enjoying the season of seasons.

His 35 League goals equalled Brian McClair's all-time record for the Premier League, and there are many who will insist that, had injury not ruled him out of the final League game of the season – against Kilmarnock – he might even have added McClair's record to his haul. Instead, he had to settle for the Golden Shoe, presented at a gala occasion in Monaco in August. And the delight was there for all to see.

'I'm very proud to win this,' he revealed. 'It's also a great reflection on my team-mates, who have been brilliant. There are so many people who share this, but I suppose people like Chris Sutton have to get a special mention. Chris is a great player and has worked so hard all season for the team and has played a big part in many of my goals.

'I said all along,' he added, 'that the most important thing was to win the League and then the Cup competitions we were in, but it's a great feeling to also be named the top striker in Europe.'

The award, and the season that brought it about, might also give Larsson the contentment he has been seeking throughout his career, at the same time indicating precisely why he is settled in this part of a world, which would appear to be his oyster.

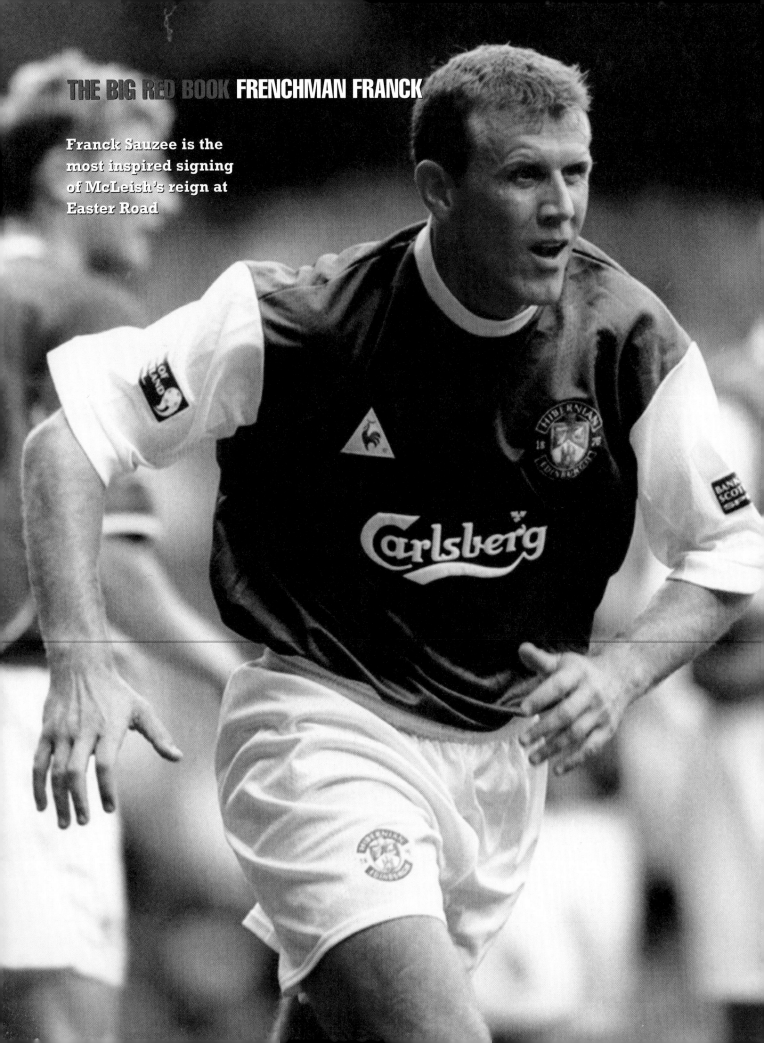

Franck Sauzee is the
most inspired signing
of McLeish's reign at
Easter Road

CHAPTER 9 FRENCHMAN FRANCK

FRENCHMAN FRANCK

Alex McLeish has embraced the idea of enlisting the Foreign Legion better than most. But the Hibs boss believes, no matter how many more players he brings in from abroad, he will never make a better signing than Frenchman Franck Sauzee.

All the more remarkable, therefore, that McLeish first persuaded the 39-times capped Gallic star to enlist in his green-and-white army while Hibs were still battling to get out of the First Division. Few could have imagined, when Sauzee signed from Montpellier towards the end of that 1998–9 season, the impact he would have on the club's rehabilitation as a Premier League outfit. It is no exaggeration to say he is the most inspired signing of McLeish's reign at Easter Road.

With three French championship medals on his CV, Sauzee has previously plied his trade at Sochaux, Marseille, Monaco, Atalanta, Strasbourg and Montpellier. His first full season in Scotland was spent helping Hibs re-establish themselves in the top flight following their brief sojourn in the First Division, but last season his class really began to shine through. He was shifted from midfield to defence by manager Alex McLeish, which proved an inspired move as he was the shining light of a

Franck Sauzee meets up with old foe Ian Durrant during a Hibs–Kilmarnock match.

Capped 39 times for France, Franck Sauzee has helped to transform Hibs' fortunes

back division that conceded only 35 League goals – a total bettered only by eventual champions Celtic.

A club that had been in turmoil two seasons before pushed Celtic all the way in the League race and, for some time, occupied the second-top slot that would have brought a Champions League placing. Sauzee was the inspiration behind the remarkable turnaround in the fortunes of the Edinburgh outfit, and, as their confidence grew, their fans began to believe again. The League campaign was ultimately to end in disappointment with a third-place finish, but Hibs also managed to reach the Scottish Cup final, going down 3–0 to Celtic at Hampden.

Of course, Franck was no stranger to these shores when he arrived. He had played for France against the national team at Hampden in 1989 in a World Cup qualifier – a game won 2–0 by Scotland that put us on the way to Italia 1990. He returned again in 1992 with Marseille to play against Rangers in the Champions League and fared slightly better, leaving Ibrox with a 2–2 draw. He did, however, get the final say, scoring Marseille's goal in a 1–1 draw in the return leg at the Velodrome. That proved enough to see the French side through to the final, when Franck picked up a winner's medal in a 1–0 win over AC Milan in Munich.

CALEY THISTLE IN NEW SCOTTISH CUP DRAMA

THERE is nothing quite like the drama of the third round of the Tennent's Scottish Cup when the big boys put themselves at the mercy of the giant killers. And, on a cold winter's afternoon in February, the excitement of our premier Cup competition was encapsulated in Inverness.

Just a year after shocking the footballing world by dumping Celtic at Parkhead – a 3–1 shock defeat that cost John Barnes his job – Caley Thistle lined up against SPL big boys Kilmarnock.

The game had swung from end to end, Killie had a goal not given when the linesman didn't see that a shot from Andy McLaren had crossed the line, and it was a classic Cup tie in every sense of the word.

In the first minute of injury time, Kilmarnock defender Gus MacPherson made a poor clearance on the edge of the box, and Caley's Barry Robson cracked a sweet shot into the bottom corner. Had Caley done it again? Was there to be another SPL scalp to add to their belt? The home fans rejoiced but, straight from the re-start, Killie went up the park and equalised when Garry Hay fired in at the back post. Victory had been snatched from the Highlanders in what was one of the most dramatic ends to a Cup tie for years.

'We were certainly fortunate to get the draw after they scored so late on,' admitted goal hero Hay. 'To be honest, you are always thinking at that stage it might be all over, but fair play to the boys, we kept our heads up and went right up the park to equalise. I was in the right place at the right time for Gus MacPherson's cross and I just slammed it into the net.'

But the drama was not finished yet as Caley Thistle tried to brave the Arctic conditions that had crippled Scotland to get to Ayrshire for the replay ten days later. They did make it, but referee Dougie McDonald had no choice but to abandon the match after just 28 minutes when it became clear players were at risk on the icy surface. The score was 0–0 when the game was abandoned so the tie rolled on for another week, with Caley heading back to Rugby Park.

Again Bobby Williamson's team looked like going out when they fell behind to their First Division opponents after 51 minutes. But Killie showed they have an abundance of character, and one player who typifies their great team spirit is Kevin McGowne. The big defender netted a rare goal to cancel out David Xausa's opener for Caley, before Paul Wright netted a penalty to take Killie through to a quarter-final tie with Hibs at home.

'I think the ball actually hit the top of my arm before going into the net,' McGowne admitted, 'but I wasn't caring one little bit and neither were the rest of the lads. To be fair to Caley Thistle, they made it difficult for us and there wasn't much between the teams over 180 minutes of football. But we're in the next round and that is all that counts. Now we can look forward to Hibs and, hopefully, making it through to the semi-finals.'

'I didn't think we were going to go out,' insisted Williamson. 'Remember, everything can change in a split second. It's the hardest part of the game, putting the ball in the back of the net. Look what happened at Inverness when we scored with seconds to go.'

Caley boss Steve Paterson must have spent the long bus journey back to Inverness thinking about what could have been, way back in the first game, when his team took the lead in injury time only to find out that the Cup has its heartbreaks as well as its romances.

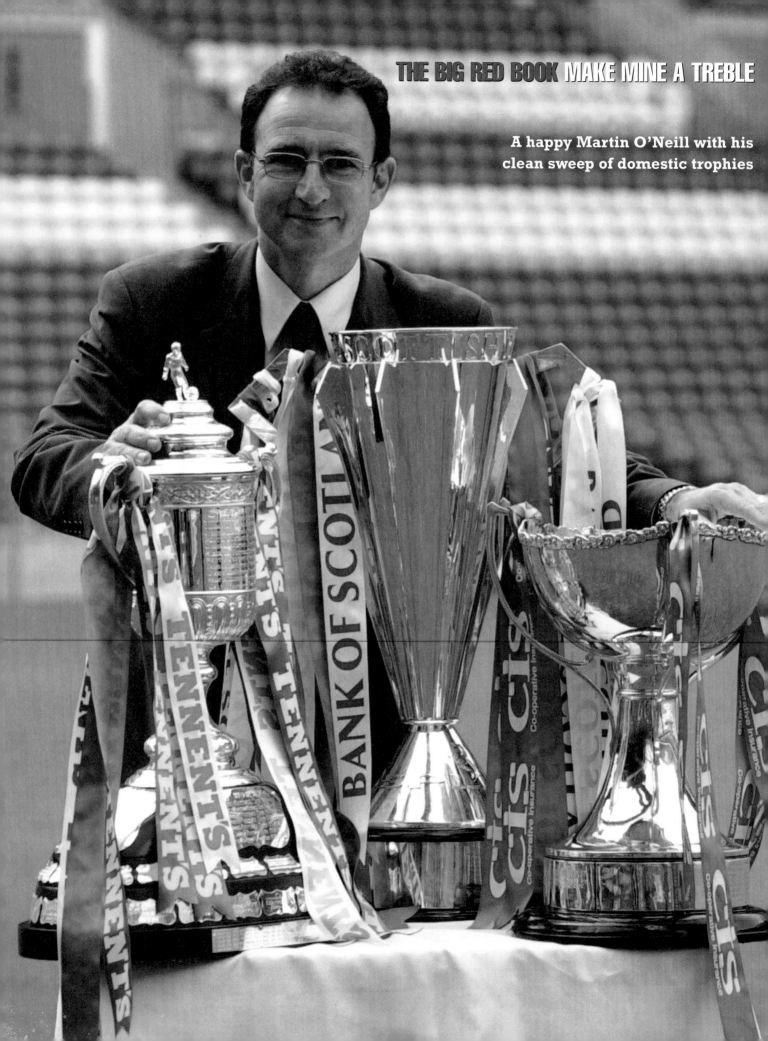

A happy Martin O'Neill with his clean sweep of domestic trophies

MAKE MINE A TREBLE

The Tennent's Scottish Cup brought down the curtain on a season filled with drama, tragedy, tears and, ultimately, joy. But the twists and turns between the start of the road to Hampden and the few steps up to the presentation platform at the national stadium can seldom have proved so difficult to negotiate. Unless you happened to have been a Celtic player, of course, whose destiny always appeared to lie in a successful conclusion to a season of wonder. And their lap of honour around Hampden on 26 May completed a treble that gave them a place in history and in the hearts of their fans across the world who had tuned in to see Martin O'Neill's side defeat Hibs 3–0.

The battle of the greens was a fitting conclusion to the season as the Parkhead side had dominated the League campaign, but Alex McLeish's emerging team had pushed them virtually all the way. The Easter Road side had promised so much, but in the end the superior quality of Celtic, and, in particular, that man Henrik Larsson, saw them finish the season

In the end the superior quality of Celtic saw them finish the season with nothing but praise to show for all their efforts

with nothing but praise to show for all their efforts.

Yet that sunny day in May must have seemed like a million light years away when the SPL sides took their first faltering steps in this year's Cup competition on icy pitches at the end of January.

The powers that be had taken it upon themselves to programme the third round of the Cup – the stage at which the lower League and non-League sides get their first chance to become giant-killers – as the opening matches for the SPL clubs after their mid-season break. So while Rangers' and Celtic's players were enjoying themselves in the January sunshine of Florida, in the back of their minds were games against Brechin and Stranraer respectively. At the same time, the minnows were living in hope that they could catch the big boys cold, literally, and cause an upset. Of course, even by this stage, many dreams of Cup glory were already lying like discarded wrapping paper from Christmas presents.

The opening two rounds had been as hard

Alloa's Derek Clarke and Aberdeen's Rachid Belabed battle for the ball in the third round of the Scottish Cup

fought as ever, with the carrot of a money-spinning glamour tie drawing that extra bit of effort from many players. Sadly, of the real giant-killers from the non-League qualifiers, only Buckie Thistle negotiated their way through to round three, removing Division Three high-fliers Hamilton in the upset of the second round. And the romantic element they brought to the competition was soon removed by Ross County who, themselves, had not so long ago been a non-League side who annually rose to prominence in the national competition.

The extremes thrown up by the Cup were never better illustrated than by Brechin, who had booked their lucrative third-round trip to Ibrox by travelling to Coldstream and defeating the East of Scotland League side 6–2. Their reward was 90 minutes against Dick Advocaat's side, who were already viewing the Scottish Cup as their best chance of silverware in a season that had promised so much only a few short months earlier. With this in mind, Rangers

> **The extremes thrown up by the Cup were never better illustrated than by Brechin**

were in no mood to indulge their visitors' dreams of Cup glory and duly dispatched them 2–0.

Likewise, Hibs ignored the fact that Easter Road was looking more like a building site than a football stadium and, like navvies, set about the task of removing Clyde, running out 6–1 winners by the end of their shift.

Their city neighbours, Hearts, met a deal more resistance in the shape of Berwick Rangers. The plucky Shielfield side battled all the way to pull off a goalless draw and force a replay that they lost only by the odd goal in three.

Of course, Berwick had already made their name as giant-killers a couple of decades earlier. And Stranraer believed they could become the 'Wee Rangers' of the new millennium when they were drawn at home against a Celtic side who would not easily be allowed to forget the fact that they had been dumped from the competition by Inverness Caley Thistle at the same stage 12 months earlier. As they ran out in front of the shock-seeking Sky TV cameras at a very chilly Stair Park, the ghost of that night was like a 12th man in the Hoops line-up. But this was duly exorcised as O'Neill's men showed all the right type of spirit to win 4–1 and cruise into round four.

There Dunfermline were waiting to present a more substantial challenge, which they delivered in the shape of a 2–2 draw at East End Park. The replay was an extra fixture Celtic could have done without, but they knuckled down and finished the job in style at Parkhead where they ran out as convincing 4–1 winners.

Hearts also needed a second game to get past Dundee 1–0, and Kilmarnock were given a huge scare at Inverness before they finally got the better of the previous season's giant-killers 2–1 in a replay at Rugby Park. Rangers were another club to have a scare in the Highlands as Ross County pushed them all the way in Dingwall before Dick Advocaat's men ran out as 3–2 winners.

Hibs were likewise made to sweat before they

> **That left two outstanding ties, one of which caused a major shock, the other producing thousands of headlines**

emerged from the mist at Forthbank as the narrowest of victors of a five-goal thriller against Stirling Albion, reported to be have been one of the best games never seen at Albion's fog-bound ground.

Dundee United also hit three, but without reply as they cruised through their tie at Motherwell. That left two outstanding ties, one of which caused a major shock, the other producing not a single shot or pass but thousands of headlines. The upset came at Pittodrie, where First Division leaders Livingston confirmed that they will be a welcome addition to the SPL by defeating Aberdeen 1–0 after their first meeting at Almondvale had finished goalless.

But this was overshadowed by the headlines generated at Airdrie when action by the liquidators only days before the Diamonds' cup tie against Peterhead forced the new Broomfield club to withdraw from the competition. Peterhead were embarrassed but found themselves handed a bye through into the quarter-finals, where they were

Celtic were up against Stranraer in the third round – a team intent on becoming the 'wee Rangers' as Paul Walker battled through against Celtic's Tom Boyd and Jackie McNamara

drawn away to Livingston. The arguments raged over whether or not Airdrie should have been allowed to remain in the Cup as the potential revenue raised from a run would obviously have helped their plight. But without enough registered players to field a side, there really was only one decision the SFA could take to protect the integrity of their flagship competition. Peterhead's good fortune was not to last much longer, as Livvy duly sent them back North with a 3–1 defeat to ponder. In the semi-final they would face Hibs, who had removed Kilmarnock 1–0, thanks to a Tom McManus goal in a tough tie at Rugby Park.

In a strange twist, the remaining two quarter-final ties were also decided by a single goal – but only one half of the Old Firm were happy about that. While Celtic squeezed past Hearts, thanks to Larsson's 43rd goal of the season at Parkhead, Rangers' campaign was coming to a shuddering halt at Tannadice. And, to rub salt in Rangers' fans'

wounds, it was ex-Celtic midfielder David Hannah who scored the goal that removed their last vestige of hope that the season could still end on a high note. Bert Konterman's dismissal had made a Rangers' comeback less than likely, and the post-mortem of a campaign that had promised so much only to deliver absolutely nothing was under way.

The semi-final draw gave United the opportunity to pull off an Old Firm double. But it turned out to be a match too much for them, and they weakly surrendered 3–1. Larsson chose the occasion to score a double and break Charlie Nicholas's 18-year-old scoring record for a Celt in a season.

Derek Lilley's late consolation was nothing more than that as, by then, Jackie McNamara had also got on the scoresheet for O'Neill's rampant side, who had already been crowned SPL champions by the time they had kicked off this semi-final. Only Hibs would stand between them

Dundee's Claudio Canigggia battles against Austin McCann of Hearts in the fourth round Cup tie

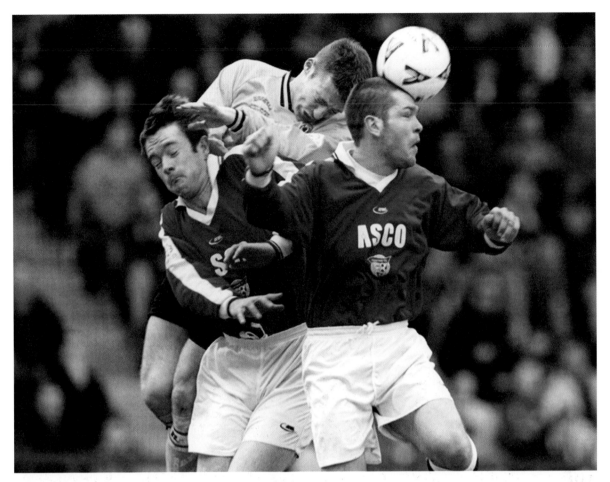

David Bingham helps to end Peterhead's Cup run as Livingston go through to the semi-finals

and the treble after the Easter Road men had ended Livingston's dreams of Cup glory with a solid 3–0 victory that had been set up by an early John O'Neil goal, secured by David Zitelli's second and delivered with another from O'Neil late on.

And so to the final on 26 May. The packed crowd were delighted to see Lubo Moravcik and Franck Sauzee run out. The talented veterans had beaten injury scares to take their places, but within 17 minutes, Moravcik's final was over as the gaping wound below his left knee had re-opened. That was the cue for sub Jackie McNamara to take over, and 21 minutes later his happiness was doubled as he became the unlikely scorer of the opening goal after excellent leading-up work by former Hibee Didier Agathe.

Three minutes after the break, McNamara turned provider, setting up Larsson to blast the ball home off his new boots, which he had changed into at the interval.

'I changed my boots at half-time,' the Swede said. 'I felt they didn't have that much grip in the first half, so I changed. They had two extra studs, so that felt great.' The same kangaroo-skin boots were to prove lethal again before the end after Larsson had been hauled down by Gary Smith in the area. Larsson picked himself up, dusted himself down and slotted home the penalty for his 53rd and final goal of the season.

Hibs manager Alex McLeish – who had gone into the game surrounded by speculation that he would soon be on his way to West Ham – was disappointed but not downhearted. He accepted that the better team had won on the day and said, 'Celtic deserved to beat us. My focus has to be on improving Hibs, and that, I am sure, we will do. I am still a young manager, and I still have much to learn.'

As for Martin O'Neill and his players, they only had to learn to say, 'We won the treble.'

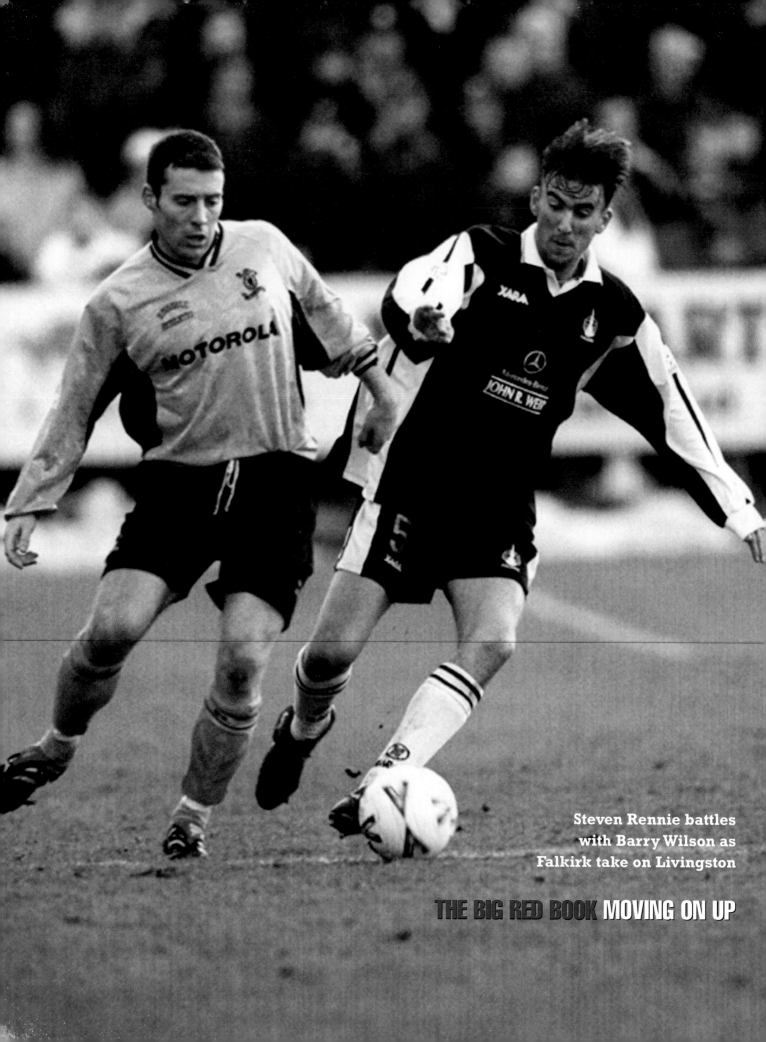

Steven Rennie battles
with Barry Wilson as
Falkirk take on Livingston

THE BIG RED BOOK MOVING ON UP

MOVING ON UP
THE FIRST, SECOND AND THIRD DIVISION TITLES

FIRST DIVISION

The fairy tale that is Livingston had a new chapter added to its amazing story when the one-time works team proved anything is possible if you put your mind to it by winning promotion to the Scottish Premier League. The scale of the achievement has been well documented, but it is worth recalling that, as recently as 1974, Ferranti Thistle (as they then were) only ever rated a mention on the odd occasion when, as an East of Scotland League club, they ventured into the very early rounds of the Scottish Cup. They were the Spartans or the Civil Service Strollers of their day.

An amazing metamorphosis has seen them transformed into a Scottish League side playing in front of a few hundred hardy souls at a wet and windy Commonwealth Stadium to a decamped team trying to bring the senior football gospel to the town of Livingston. And they are now a club who last season were only one Scottish Cup game away from earning a place in Europe and who will be rubbing shoulders with the Old Firm throughout this season.

> **'I feel this is not just a great day for Livingston but for the people of West Lothian'**

All this has been achieved through hard work, sound investment and a belief that dreams do come true. Under the guidance of chairman Dominic Keane and coaching supremos Jim Leishman and Davie Hay, Livvy's Lions have roared like no one would have thought possible a couple of years ago. And after they got their claws into last season's First Division championship, it soon became clear that there was no way they were going to give it up without a fight. Not even early setbacks against more fancied promotion hopefuls Raith Rovers and Falkirk could unhinge Livvy's belief that the side that had done so well in their debut season in the First Division could go all the way this time around. They believed they had bought well to strengthen the squad, and, over the course of a testing season, that proved to be the case.

Tight at the back and deadly up front, they had the basis of a winning side. The confidence instilled in them by old warhorses Leishman and Hay, both of whom have managed successfully at the very highest level, helped keep everyone focused when main challengers such as Ayr and Falkirk got close.

Livingston manager Jim Leishman – the hero of West Lothian

In the end, the championship was won by an impressive seven points, despite a last-day defeat at the hands of Clyde that put a slight – but only slight – dampener on the celebrations at Almondvale. By then, the hard work had been done, and the dream of taking on the big boys had become reality. But the honours did not end there. The bard of Scottish football, Leishman, was crowned First Division Manager of the Year, while striker David Bingham deservedly lifted the players' award. Leishman was happy to take the prize, but he does not underestimate the job done by men like Hay and coach John Robertson and those who went before them, like former boss Ray Stewart.

'What Livingston have achieved is history,' he insisted. 'To go from the Third Division, to the Second, to the First, and then the Premier League is something no other club in Scotland has ever achieved. I feel this is not just a great day for Livingston but for the people of West Lothian. There are thousands affected by the Motorola

The Livingston bench erupts as the final whistle sounds and promotion is won

Livingston celebrate as the Premiership dream becomes reality

closure. This will not help them pay the bills, but hopefully, in some small way, it will have cheered them up. Are we going to stay up? I'm not going to answer that right now. Today is not about that, it is about the players.'

The success of Livingston with its impressive stadium was also a relief to the SPL officials, who had ruled that, of all the promotion challengers, only Livvy would be granted entry to the top division as the grounds of the others did not reach an acceptable standard. Once again, this is testimony to the forward-thinking and good housekeeping of the club, who are expected to become a real asset to the SPL, especially after further adding to their player base during the summer.

They have already proved that they can compete against the top sides, their Scottish Cup run taking them all the way to the semi-finals where they lost to Hibs 3–0. Victory would have given them a place in the final against Celtic and automatic entry to the UEFA Cup as the Parkhead side were already qualified for the Champions League. But, nice though that would have been, the

main objective was always to win the First Division title, and it was mission accomplished on 28 April thanks to a 3–2 win at Inverness.

On the same day, Morton and the only part-time side in the division, Alloa, also left the division, although they were headed in the opposite direction from Livvy after losing their battles against relegation.

For Morton, it was the latest in a long line of disasters as the club's financial plight worsened by the week. The long-running takeover by English businessman Mike Peden had already fallen through, and the man he had put in place as manager, Allan Evans, had been removed. As the Cappielow ground continued to decay, the Morton fans feared the roof was about to fall in on the club, too, as the administrators took over the day-to-day running of the club – and sacked all the staff.

Morton were not the only club to play most of the season under the watchful eye of administrators. Airdrie, who had hoped that the emergence of Steve Archibald in July 2000 as the preferred bidder for the troubled club would mark the beginning of the end of their problems, slowly but surely discovered that this was not to be the case. And by February, Archibald found himself locked out of New Broomfield as the liquidators moved in.

The Diamonds had to release almost all their players, forcing them to withdraw from the Scottish Cup and postpone all League games for over five weeks until Ian McCall had been appointed manager by Jim Innes, who had taken over interim control of the club. It was a relief that the Diamonds were able to fulfil their fixtures and amazing that they managed to avoid relegation after McCall had to sign an entire team, but it was also a painful reminder to almost every other club in Scotland that the economics of survival can no longer be ignored.

SECOND DIVISION

It's not very often that the Scottish Second Division can claim a first. But thanks to Partick Thistle's amazing runaway success last season, it managed to do just that. The Jags became the first side in Britain to clinch promotion, and they had sewn it up by the final day in March. That's faster than even one of manager John Lambie's pigeons, but in typical Thistle style they then made their fans sweat for weeks before actually going on to clinch the championship.

The truth is, Lambie's side could afford to take their foot off the gas and coast to the title, such an impressive lead had they established over the pack left trailing in their wake. And it came in the most unlikely of circumstances. A 2–2 draw against struggling Forfar at Station Park looked, on the face of it, to be a disappointing result. Until, that is, the news filtered through that the only club standing between them and hoisting the flag, Arbroath, had lost 1–0 to Queen of the South at Palmerston, handing the title to the Jags. Not the way Lambie had planned it, but welcome relief nevertheless and thoroughly deserved.

The veteran manager, who had previously led Thistle to the higher echelons of the Premier League, was delighted to have turned the Jags around.

'This is absolutely tremendous,' he said. 'Our supporters have waited two or three years for this, and I am pleased for them when you look at the large number who have travelled here. That is one job done. Now we have to look ahead to next

John Lambie with Partick Thistle's Championship trophy

Partick Thistle celebrate with the Championship trophy

Jubilation in the Partick camp after clinching the title

season to see if we can move forward from here. There are seven steps to heaven, and we are only on the third one. But this matches anything I have achieved before, although it is not about John Lambie. The players are the ones who have got us to this stage.'

Yet, in the first few weeks of the season, there had been little to indicate that Thistle were going to be so dominant. Their trademark enigmatic performances had exposed their potential. But their fans had had their appetite whetted by this before, only to finish the season sick to their stomachs as other sides had proved hungrier to make the step up. Once Lambie got them into top gear, however, there was to be no stopping the Jags' bandwagon. One by one, they steam-rollered their promotion rivals until there emerged a clear route back to the First Division. At the final count, Thistle had won the title by an impressive 17 points from Arbroath who, in turn, finished four points clear of Berwick and Stranraer.

It was a job well done by Lambie, and he revealed that getting them back on an upward spiral after plummeting down the divisions amid serious financial problems was just one of his objectives. 'Putting a smile back on the face of this club was just about as important,' insisted the Jags manager.

'It's what I've enjoyed most since coming back – seeing people going about smiling. This place was dead when I came back, and that was one thing I wanted to put right. It's about everyone related to the club – the office staff, the kitmen, everybody. Mind you, it's come a year earlier than I thought it would.'

With some justification, Clydebank will probably believe they could have mounted more of a challenge had they not had to cope with the serious handicaps of administration and homelessness. To finish in fifth place, having taken points off all the promotion-chasing sides, was a creditable performance of which their small band of loyal fans should be proud.

Certainly, the supporters of relegated pair Stirling Albion and Queen's Park must wish their teams had shown as much fight. The Forthbank club in particular were a huge disappointment and always looked destined for the drop. Queen's Park, on the other hand, hadn't looked to be in any danger until the closing few weeks, when Forfar started to claw their way to safety. The point against champions Thistle, plus victories over Stirling then Queen's Park on the final day, saw Station Park retain Second Division status.

But while there was much disappointment for the two relegated teams, there was much to celebrate at Firhill and also at Gayfield where the Red Lichties proved a surprise package to many. They won fewer than half their 36 League matches, but they won when it mattered most and brought First Division football back to Arbroath after a long absence.

THIRD DIVISION

The battle to get out of Scottish football's basement division is always keenly contested. And, with little by way of resources, it often takes as much good luck as good football to win promotion. When last

Ally Dawson holds the Championship trophy aloft as the Accies kiss the Third Division goodbye

season's Third Division kicked off, however, Hamilton Accies reckoned they had a distinct advantage over their 11 opponents. They believed they should never have been down there in the first place, and, while many clubs reckon they are playing beneath their ability, in this case Accies had a point. Or rather, they didn't have 15 points, which was what cost them their Second Division status in the first place. The deduction of 15 points for failing to fulfil a fixture because of a players' protest over the non-payment of wages had been a penalty too hard to bear, and, ultimately, it saw them relegated at the end of season 1999–2000. Had they not been so severely punished, they would have finished the season in a mid-table position.

It was a bitter pill to swallow for the homeless heroes who previously thrilled Hamilton fans at the now demolished Douglas Park. But manager Ally Dawson wisely decided to turn adversity to advantage as he got his troops to rally behind the flag of injustice. And, despite some shaky spells through the hard-fought campaign, Dawson was able to lead them triumphantly to the League championship. Ultimately, they only lifted the title on goal difference from Cowdenbeath. But that was fitting, as Dawson's side had been the top scorers in the division, had conceded fewer goals than anyone else and had also lost fewer games than their 11 competitors. This rise back up the divisions could not be better timed, as Accies now have a new stadium, New Douglas Park, within a long throw-in of their spiritual home, the old and much loved original Douglas Park.

After making an assured and impressive start to life in the Third Division, however, they had to wait until the last week of the season before they could guarantee Second Division football would grace the new ground. And, by coincidence, it was back-to-back victories over Montrose in the space of four days that gave them promotion and then the title. They defeated the Links Park side in a rearranged midweek game and followed that up with another victory on the final weekend as the other two sides vying for promotion, Cowdenbeath and Brechin, went head-to-head.

Former Rangers' defender Dawson was in no doubt how important the achievement was.

'This is one of the proudest moments of my career,' he said. 'I am not kidding when I say the

The Accies celebrate their return to Division Two

feeling I've got from this title win is right up there with anything I achieved at Rangers. When you see the 700 people who have followed us up the road to Montrose and how much it means to them, I think it's safe to say there are good times ahead at the new stadium.'

The race to join Accies on the way up went all the way to the wire before long-time leaders Cowdenbeath emerged as short-head winners over City, courtesy of a 2–1 win that sent Central Park into a frenzy. It was a great relief to the Blue Brazil, who had staggered and stumbled towards the finishing line.

They also had to overcome their own major internal problems midway through the season when Craig Levein quit as manager to take over at Hearts. The hot seat was offered to Peter Cormack, but he was deposed after only ten days in the job and before even leading them into a single game. So it was left to Gary Kirk to steady the ship and steer Cowdenbeath to the Second Division.

No matter how anxious and worried their fans had been, however, they at least got the result they longed for, unlike the supporters of Brechin City, who must go through it all over again this season. And they know the competition will be every bit as hot, not least because the new boys who made their bow in senior football last season, Elgin and Peterhead, are sure to be that bit more streetwise.

Dumbarton, now accustomed to their new Strathclyde Homes Stadium, which saw Paddy Flannery score the first competitive goal there in the 2–0 win over Elgin in December, will also expect to build on what was a season of some promise.

Demoted sides Queen's Park and Stirling Albion will also make it tough for Brechin and the rest. But at least they know they were relegated because they did not win enough points and, determined though they will be to return to the Second Division, they will not carry with them the special incentive to bounce back up that Hamilton brought with them last season.

A TOUCH OF KAMIKAZE

THEY DID their best, this current lot, but ultimately they almost lived up to the traditions of their forefathers, who were always capable of snatching defeat from the jaws of victory.

It was always thus. There is a suicidal tendency inherent in the character of Scotland sides. It's as though we wish to raise hopes and dreams only to crush them into the turf of stadiums throughout the world. Nothing much changes, and although the 2–2 draw with Belgium at Hampden over the weekend should not be regarded as any kind of disaster in terms of qualification, it was a glorious opportunity tossed to the winds of happenstance.

Over the past 48 hours Craig Brown has been attempting to analyse the reasons for his team's failure to capitalise upon a major and early advantage. He has taken an upbeat approach, stating that his squad can, and will, travel to the Far East for the finals. Quietly, however, he must be aware this was a wonderful opportunity tossed away.

The essence of success at the highest level of football is to take full advantage of home fixtures. Although the Belgians travelled to Glasgow with a decent pedigree, they were by no means insurmountable opposition.

Dodds struck with a goal of the highest quality. It was inventive – as clever as you could wish to see on any international occasion. Clearly galvanised, the Scots were operating to the peak of their abilities. Burley's corner-kick found Hendry, who rose above the Belgian defence and sent in the header that was handled on the goal line by Eric Deflandre. It was a clear penalty and Dodds sent his shot high into the net. Deflandre was red-carded, the automatic punishment for being the last man in a defence to handle the ball. And so the Scots appeared to be in complete control.

The conclusion should have been secured shortly after the interval when Dominic Matteo powered down the left side and found Barry Ferguson with an accurate, low cross. The Rangers captain went in against the goalkeeper but shot the ball into his body from just eight yards. It was then suspicions of impending gloom began to loom large.

Belgium had brought on their towering substitute, Bob Peeters, for the second half and he sent over a cross from the left where the excellent Marc Wilmots, unmarked, struck a ten-yard header wide of Neil Sullivan. As the tension within the crowd became almost palpable, and as Belgium grew in confidence, Scotland were on the back foot.

Two minutes after normal time, just when it seemed the three points had been secured, the entire ball game changed. Vanderhaeghe's cross was punishing, leaving the Scottish defence guessing over its intent. Daniel van Buyten did not, however, suffer any sense of hesitancy as, from ten yards and again unmarked, he sent his header high past the flailing left hand of Sullivan.

And so the Scots exited, overwhelmed by a sense of despair. Elementary errors contributed to the loss of what may well prove to be two significant points. Brown could hardly contain his anger at seeing precious points slip away, although he is adamant that there can be an exercise in damage limitation.

'I thought that for the entirety of the first half we played very well. When we were a couple of goals ahead we were confident, although I told the players at half-time that nothing was guaranteed. We could have had everything tied up in the second half before the Belgians dragged themselves back into the game. For them to equalise so late was a huge blow, but working with my players and recognising their resilience I know they will pick themselves up for Wednesday's game with San Marino.'

If only the Scots had not once more pressed the self-destruct button they would by now have been pencilling in the journey to the Far East.

THE SHAMING
OF SCOTLAND'S CAPTAIN

IF THE GAME is not entirely burst then surely it is terminally flawed. **On the field and off it Scotland has discarded notions of decency and intelligence.**

At Hampden on Wednesday the captain of the national side, Colin Hendry, committed what would be regarded by the Scottish courts as a clear case of serious assault on a young San Marino player, Nicola Albani. He refused to apologise in the aftermath, although later he did become just a touch penitent.

The entire episode was an illustration of a malaise that is threatening to destroy the game of football as we have come to know it. In a matter of seconds – during which Hendry connected twice with his elbow on Albani – the structure and territory of the game were placed in a microcosm. Here we had a lad of 19 who was trying to do his best for a tiny republic on the north-east coast of Italy. Here, again, we had a footballer, the captain of Scotland, who has earned fortunes in his career at Manchester City, Blackburn Rovers and Rangers.

Craig Brown did not cover himself in even a hint of glory yesterday as he attempted to quantify Hendry's outrageous behaviour in the final minute of a World Cup qualifier which the Scots had won 4–0. Just how he attempted to allow Hendry to become as much of a sinned party as a sinner beggars belief.

The manager is one of the finest people you will find within this business, but he let himself down big time as he attempted to rationalise Hendry's actions. He spoke of 'mitigating circumstances' when he should have been declaring Hendry a non-combatant for the future. That decision, of course, is likely to be taken out of his hands because FIFA will examine the evidence and declare him to be guilty.

As question upon question poured upon him, his position changed and he admitted, 'I do have the power of selection for the remainder of the World Cup qualifying process.'

'The player has been vilified,' he went on, 'and what I wish to do is to explain the causes and not to give you excuses. You must remember this was a super-charged atmosphere, so how do you react when you are being held back time after time, as Hendry was, when he was trying to do his best for us?'

Really, the manager should have quit when he was ahead – and that was within the first 30 seconds of his explanation. The rest of his analysis was pretty boring. He spoke of Hendry's character, of the fact it was outwith his nature to inflict injury upon an opposition player, of the way the Scotland players had been treated by San Marino and of the right of his players to respond to physical challenges. He also spoke of Hendry's second-hand apologies that had been relayed to him, although the SFA chief executive, David Taylor, was marked absent in any condemnation of one of the most shameful episodes in the history of our game.

Last night, ostensibly anyway, Brown and Taylor had not spoken about their captain's disgraceful behaviour, despite the threat of the legal authorities becoming involved. This sad and sorry incident should never have arisen. Now that it has, Hendry might well discover that his international career is over after 51 caps. The end should not have been so ungracious.

Scotland's Craig Burley
is held back by Croatia's
Stjepan Tomas

SCOTLAND
AND THE WORLD CUP FINALS

Scotland's love affair with the World Cup has never been more passionate. But, after a qualifying campaign which began with so much hope and ended with so much despair, it will be a case of absence makes the heart grow fonder when the finals kick off in Japan and South Korea next summer.

Craig Brown's eighth – and ultimately final – year in charge of the national side had begun on the back of failure to book a place in the finals of the European Championships in Belgium and Holland. Losing a play-off to get there was bad enough. Losing it to England – despite winning the second leg at Wembley – just rubbed salt into the wounds.

As ever, however, this pain and disappointment served only to strengthen the Scottish resolve to make it to the big one – the World Cup finals two years down the line. So it was with minds full of optimism, hearts full of hope and a squad full of experienced, if not brilliant players, that Scotland took their first steps on what they prayed would be a straightforward road to the 2002 finals.

Our Group Six opponents would clearly provide some formidable obstacles enroute. Croatia had, after all, finished in third place in the 1998 finals in France when that fledgling nation, born out of the fragmentation of the Balkan states, made a mockery of the fact it has a population of only six million to draw from.

The qualifying campaign, which began with so much hope, had ended with so much despair

They were quickly installed as favourites to take the single qualifying place from the group, leaving the rest to fight for the runners-up spot that brought with it a play-off place. Minnows San Marino could be instantly subtracted from the equation, while Scotland had already proved in the qualifying group for France '98 that they knew how to overcome Latvia. Which left regular adversaries Belgium as Scotland's main challengers for the position of team most likely to push Croatia all the way.

A good start was essential for all concerned. And, on 2 September 2000, Scotland emerged as the country who flew off the blocks. While Belgium and Croatia fought out a dull, goalless draw in Brussels, the Tartan Army were being entertained to a Scotland victory in Latvia. Rangers' Neil McCann got the all-important goal to further

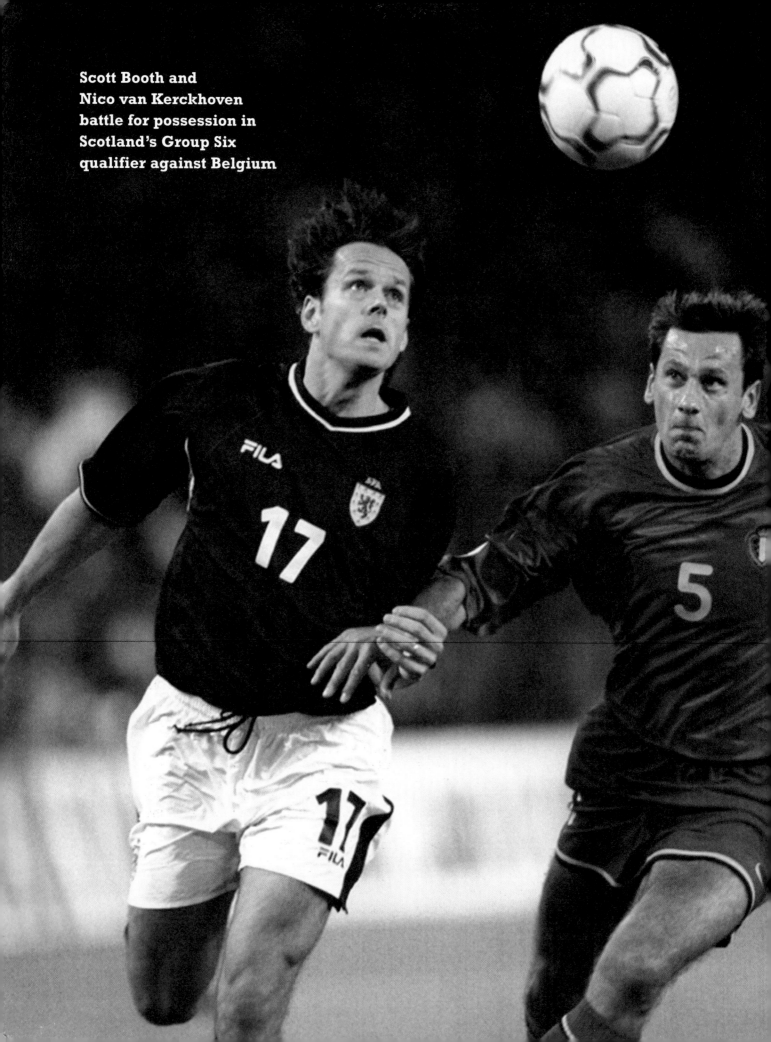

Scott Booth and
Nico van Kerckhoven
battle for possession in
Scotland's Group Six
qualifier against Belgium

enhance Scotland's growing reputation as a side capable of having successful away days. The fact that the goal arrived in the final minute was of no importance to anyone connected with the jubilant Scottish camp. The important thing was that the points were secured, and plans to turn Tokyo tartan were already being hatched. Forget the fact this was only the first game – who could stop Scotland now? Certainly not San Marino in their next match the following month.

The trip to the tiny principality set high on a hilltop in Italy was looked upon by the Tartan Army as a bit of a holiday with a Scotland victory thrown in for entertainment. The only questions to be answered were: how good was the local beer?; what presents to bring back?; and how many goals would Scotland rattle in? Well, the brew was good, the gifts probably less so, and the margin of victory acceptable, though not spectacular. And once again Scotland left it late before goals from Matt Elliott and Don Hutchison averted an embarrassing stalemate.

Finding the net was already proving to be a problem for Brown's side. But without a Denis Law, Kenny Dalglish or Charlie Nicholas to lead the line, settling for victories, however low-scoring, would have to do. The significance of goal-difference was already beginning to loom large, with Belgium winning 4–0 in Latvia the same day. Still, Scotland remained top of the group, and a 100 per cent record after two games – both away – was just what Brown wanted as he prepared his side for the first real test of the campaign, a trip to Zagreb where the Croats lay in wait.

Croatia had enjoyed a free weekend while Scotland had been toiling in San Marino. With only four days in which to recover, Brown's players would surely be at an extra disadvantage. Not for the first time, however, the Scots were to defy the odds, bamboozle the experts and stun the Croatians.

They trailed to an Alan Boksic goal when veteran striker Kevin Gallacher got behind the Croatian defence to knock home the equaliser. The goal did much to lighten the mood of coach Brown, who by then had been banished to the stand following an altercation with the match officials. He was waiting in the dressing room to welcome his players, but their mood told him they were a little disappointed as they felt they had done enough to take all three points. Nevertheless, the draw – and seven points from their opening three games – gave them genuine cause for optimism as they contemplated the resumption of the qualifying programme the following spring. The only other game played before the break saw Latvia take their first points with a 1–0 victory in San Marino. From their lofty position atop the section, Scotland could almost see Japan and South Korea. But there was some treacherous terrain to negotiate before they could set foot in the promised land.

Before Scotland could get back into action, Belgium caused something of a sensation when they pulverised San Marino 10–1 in Brussels. Who said there were no easy games left in international football? The astonishing result fired them to the top of the group on goal difference – surprise, surprise. Scotland's inability to find the net with the frequency their play often deserved was looking more and more like an albatross around Brown's neck.

> **From their lofty position atop the section, Scotland could almost see Japan and South Korea**

The Scotland manager – who realised, with his contract up for renewal at the end of the year, that his career at the helm could not withstand any more qualification failures – attempted to maintain an aura of calm. Rather than worry what others in the group might be doing to one another, Brown preferred to concentrate on what he could do with Scotland. After all, their destiny was still in their own hands. And the crucial period of the qualifying programme was just around the corner.

First up was a visit by the Belgians. Celtic defender Joos Valgaeren found himself at the centre of the media circus as he was repeatedly asked to preview the game in which he would be lining up against Billy Dodds, Don Hutchison and the rest of Scotland's would-be scorers. Diplomatically, the big defender said all the right things about the team representing his adopted home, but deep down he had high hopes he would be one of the few in Scotland still smiling after this crunch clash on 24 March.

Valgaeren had been an interested spectator as Australia had visited Hampden in November and left with a 2–0 victory. The Belgian theory was that what the Socceroos could do, the Waloons could match. They were shocked, therefore, to find themselves two goals and one man down midway through the first half.

Billy Dodds – fourth-choice striker with Rangers but first choice with his country – was the man who inflicted the killer touch so lacking in previous games. He stole in ahead of a bemused Valgaeren to fire a right-wing cross from Craig Burley into the Belgian net. And, when Eric Deflandre was adjudged to have pushed a goal-bound header away with his hand as he defended a post at a corner kick – gaining the unlucky Belgian a red card and Scotland a penalty – dead-eye Dodds stepped forward to slam home the spot-kick. Job done, or so the ecstatic home support believed.

However, only half the story had been told. And by the end of the match the predicted ending had been altered beyond all recognition. Opportunities to put the match beyond the reach of the Belgians were squandered. This gave the visitors – who by then had removed Valgaeren from the fray to spare him any further embarrassment – renewed hope. The wily and wizened Marc Wilmots rang the first alarm bell when he stole in to make it 2–1. All eyes were on the clock as a comfortable victory suddenly became a desperate siege.

In stoppage time it was the hearts of the Scotland supporters which stopped as the Belgians launched one last attack. Rising highest in the box was the giant frame of substitute Daniel van Buyten, and he redirected the ball beyond the helpless Neil Sullivan in the home goal. The final whistle was met by boos and disbelief that, not for the first time, Scotland had managed to snatch a draw from the jaws of victory. No one could say for certain how damaging that blow would prove to be. But already the feeling was that it could be fatal.

Brown had to work fast to lift the spirits of his players. After all, they had to face San Marino only four days later. That was a night for true Scots to stand up and be counted. Skipper Colin Hendry promised to lead by example. And, true to his word, he made his mark. Unfortunately in more ways than one.

Before the Belgian game, the big, burly, blond

No one could say for certain how damaging that blow would prove to be

Braveheart had collected his medal for winning 50 caps. Against San Marino he collected two goals, notoriety and a six-game ban which was later halved on appeal. His first double for his country came from two well-placed shots. Dodds added to his increasingly-impressive goal tally with another, to send Scotland in at the break on course for the sort of haul which would negate Belgium's impressive double-figures score against the group's whipping boys. Sadly, all the Scots had to show for their second-half efforts was a Colin Cameron goal. And, as the clock ticked down, the frustration increased.

Breaking point came in the dying moments when San Marino sent on teenager Nicola Albani for his first international appearance. Unfortunately for him it lasted only as long as it took Hendry to swing his elbow three times. The youngster had raced on to the field to take up position marking the Scotland skipper at a corner. But his over-eager attempts to get a grip on Hendry – literally – were not well received. The Bolton defender's final flying elbow made contact with Albani's throat and, while play raged on, the substitute lay on the ground seemingly unconscious.

The inexperienced referee had missed the incident. But the multitude of TV cameras showing the match live did not. As the game fizzled out, the furore gained momentum. Albani was rushed to hospital as Hendry was ushered into a post-match interview. In the misguided belief that the youngster had been feigning injury, Hendry's lack of remorse reflected badly on him and his position as skipper. By the time he had had a chance to see the incident on video and review his position, it was too late. The damage had been done to his reputation and to Albani's throat.

While the young San Marino player recovered to play out the remainder of the qualifying games, Hendry did not. FIFA moved swiftly to hammer him with a six-game ban. On later appeal – supported by the SFA – this was reduced to three. But it was still enough to mark the end of Hendry's involvement in the qualifying games and, at this advanced stage of his career, probably the end of his eight-year international journey. His presence would be sadly missed, not least in Scotland's next qualifying match against Croatia at Hampden in September.

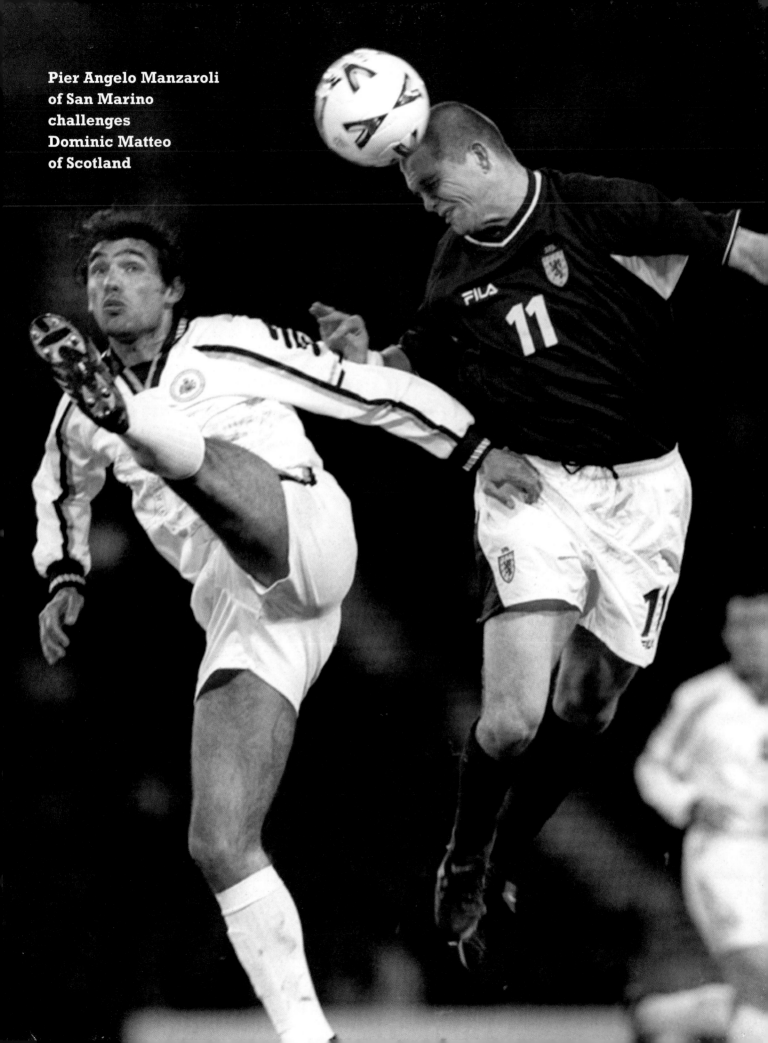

Pier Angelo Manzaroli
of San Marino
challenges
Dominic Matteo
of Scotland

Gary Naysmith takes on Belgium's Gert Verheyen at the King Baudouin Stadium

Robert Prosinecki and his team-mates had maintained their momentum in the group with a 4–1 home win over Latvia a few hours after Scotland had drawn with Belgium. And, while Scotland had settled for some down time towards the end of their domestic season – a period when our players are traditionally showing their poorest form after a long, hard campaign – the other four countries went about their business with gusto. San Marino gained their first point with a draw in Latvia – that man Albani recovering well enough to net the visitors' goal. Croatia defeated San Marino 4–0 at home, Belgium won 3–1 in Brussels against Latvia, the Latvians then lost 1–0 at home to Croatia, and, finally, Belgium emerged from San Marino with a 4–1 victory. That left Belgium three points clear at the top of the group, with Croatia and Scotland tied on 11 points behind them. Latvia's four points and San Marino's solitary one told its own story.

Craig Brown, meanwhile, had arranged a friendly in Poland for his side. Only it was not the instantly-recognisable Scotland team which took the field in the mining town of Bydgoszcz. In fact, seven players earned their first caps and helped achieve a creditable 1–1 draw that April evening.

Twente Enschede's Scott Booth was the man to emerge with most plaudits, scoring the equalising penalty and staking a claim for a place in the end-game of the much more important World Cup-qualifying programme. And sure enough, when September came around, Brown gave the former Aberdeen striker his chance in the side that lined up against Croatia at Hampden. He was selected in preference to Dodds, who was still struggling to get a starting place in the Rangers side.

As it was, Dodds replaced Booth late in the second half. But his luck in front of goal was just as dismal. The Ibrox hero did get the ball into the net inside the last five minutes, only to be ruled offside as a game, which had been dominated by the Croats in the opening 30 minutes, petered out to a goalless draw. The Croats left the field the happier band of players as Brown's men could feel their qualifying chance slipping through their fingers. Now it was a win-or-bust trip to Belgium four days later that would decide their destiny.

The former Heysel Stadium – now rebuilt and renamed the King Baudouin Stadium – had never

Brown's men could feel their qualifying chance slipping through their fingers

been a happy hunting ground for the Scots. But when they ran out there on 5 September they were fighting for the moment and the future, not wallowing in the past. Almost 15,000 Scotland fans had made the journey to lend their support, recognising their country needed them in their hour-and-a-half of need. What they needed more than anything, however, was someone to stick the ball in the net. But from early on, carving out a chance – let alone converting it – had all the indications of being a task too testing.

For all the promptings in midfield from Paul Lambert; for all the last-gasp blocks at the back by Matt Elliott; for all the willing running up front by Dodds and Hutchison, the Belgians were never truly troubled. Which was why the opening goal from Nico van Kerkhoven always looked as though it would be enough to give the home side the win they needed to set up a winner-takes-all shoot-out with Croatia in the final game of the group. As it was, Belgium's advantage was doubled in injury time when Bart Goor raced clear of the goal-chasing Scotland defence to make it 2–0.

The blue and white paint on the faces of the Scotland fans was streaked by tears as the realisation hit home. The next World Cup finals would be missing one of its regular patrons. Sure, some sort of miracle in the final games could still throw out a life-line in the shape of a play-off place. But neither Croatia nor Belgium appeared to be in the mood to hand out any second chances.

The Croats made no mistakes in their penultimate match, winning 4–0 in San Marino. They knew a win over Belgium in the concluding game would bring them their ticket to the finals. Belgium were equally confident they could get the point they needed in Zagreb to win the group and avoid a hazardous play-off. Scotland were left to hope the Belgians' confidence was not misplaced. But even if the Croatians lost their final game, Scotland would have to knock at least seven goals past Latvia at Hampden to snatch the play-off place. Having only scored ten goals in their previous seven qualifying games, it was a bit too much to ask – even for Scotland. And the mountain facing Scotland would also have to be scaled without some of their most experienced campaigners, as long-term first-picks Paul

Craig Burley muscles a Latvian defender off the ball as Dougie Freedman looks on

Barry Nicholson in action during the 2–1 win over Latvia at Hampden

Lambert, Billy Dodds and Tom Boyd decided to call time on their international careers.

Added to the usual batch of call-offs, it opened the door for some new faces to step in. As ever, though, the Brown watchword was caution and, when the Scotland side stepped out at Hampden on 6 October, only one new cap was won, Dougie Freedman stepping up from leading the line with Crystal Palace to be handed the role of shooting Scotland to the World Cup finals.

Freedman did manage to mark his début with a goal, but not until Latvia had shot down any lingering hopes retained by the ultra optimists by opening the scoring through Andrejs Rubins after a monumental blunder by Christian Dailly. Not even defender David Weir's first goal for his country shortly after the interval could spark Scotland towards the goal rush they so badly needed. They hung on to win 2–1. But ultimately it made no difference. As a dejected Scotland side trooped off the Hampden pitch, word had already reached them that Croatia had defeated Belgium 1–0 to win the group and collect the golden ticket to Japan and South Korea.

The Belgians were almost as disappointed as the Scots. They had gone into the final day's qualifying programme at the top of the group, knowing a draw would carry them to the finals. But this defeat put them into a play-off, with the Czech Republic between them and the World Cup finals draw on 1 December. While Croatia and Belgium looked to distant horizons, Scotland could only look inward, wondering how their stock had managed to sink so far down that they were now listed 48th in the FIFA rankings – an all-time low. Of more importance was how they were going to lift themselves again.

Whatever the answer to that, Craig Brown would not be part of it. Within minutes of overseeing his 70th game in charge of Scotland, he stepped down as national coach. Thanking his players, his employers and the fans for their support throughout his time in charge, he said his farewells and departed the stage. Who would now take the leading role at the heart of the Scottish game was a question the SFA had to answer quickly. But, of equal importance, they knew they had to find the right solution to restore a nation's heart. After all, the qualifying programme for the 2004 European Championships is less than a year away . . .

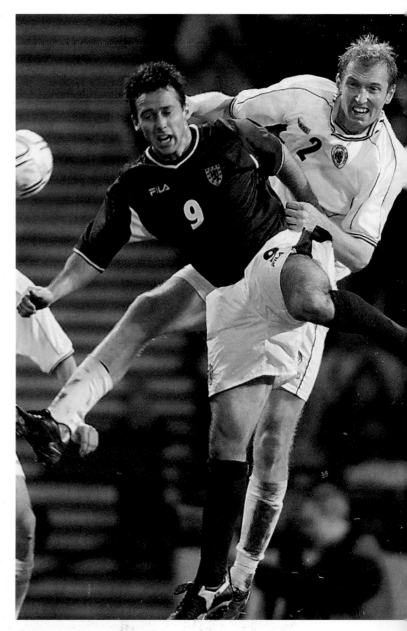

Good ... but not good enough

GROUP SIX RESULTS

	P	W	D	L	F	A	Pt
Croatia	8	5	3	0	15	2	18
Belgium	8	5	2	1	25	6	17
Scotland	8	4	3	1	12	6	15
Latvia	8	1	1	6	5	16	4
San Marino	8	0	1	7	3	30	1

THE SCOREBOARD

SCOTTISH PREMIERSHIP LEAGUE RESULTS

Aberdeen

Dunfermline 0 Aberdeen 0
Aberdeen 2 St Mirren 1
Aberdeen 1 Hearts 1
Rangers 4 Aberdeen 2
Aberdeen 0 Hibs 2
Motherwell 1 Aberdeen 1
Aberdeen 1 St Johnstone 1
Kilmarnock 1 Aberdeen 0
Dundee Utd 3 Aberdeen 5
Aberdeen 1 Celtic 1
Aberdeen 0 Dundee 2
Aberdeen 0 Dunfermline 0
St Mirren 2 Aberdeen 0
Hearts 3 Aberdeen 0
Aberdeen 1 Rangers 2
Hibs 0 Aberdeen 2
Aberdeen 3 Motherwell 3
St Johnstone 0 Aberdeen 0
Aberdeen 1 Kilmarnock 2
Aberdeen 4 Dundee Utd 1
Celtic 6 Aberdeen 0
Dundee 2 Aberdeen 2
Dunfermline 3 Aberdeen 2
Aberdeen 3 St Mirren 0
Aberdeen 1 Hearts 0
Rangers 1 Aberdeen 0
Aberdeen 1 Hibs 0
Motherwell 0 Aberdeen 1
Aberdeen 3 St Johnstone 3
Kilmarnock 0 Aberdeen 0
Dundee United 1 Aberdeen 1
Aberdeen 0 Celtic 1
Aberdeen 0 Dundee 2
Aberdeen 1 Dunfermline 0
St Johnstone 0 Aberdeen 3
Motherwell 0 Aberdeen 2
St Mirren 2 Aberdeen 1
Aberdeen 1 Dundee Utd 2

Celtic

Dundee United 1 Celtic 2
Celtic 1 Motherwell 0
Celtic 2 Kilmarnock 1
St Johnstone 0 Celtic 2
Hearts 2 Celtic 4
Celtic 6 Rangers 2
Celtic 3 Hibs 0
Dunfermline 1 Celtic 2
Celtic 1 Dundee 0
Aberdeen 1 Celtic 1
Celtic 2 St Mirren 0
Celtic 2 Dundee Utd 1
Motherwell 3 Celtic 3
Kilmarnock 0 Celtic 1
Celtic 4 St Johnstone 1
Celtic 6 Hearts 1
Rangers 5 Celtic 1
Hibs 0 Celtic 0
Celtic 3 Dunfermline 1
Dundee 1 Celtic 2
Celtic 6 Aberdeen 0
St Mirren 0 Celtic 2
Dundee Utd 0 Celtic 4
Celtic 1 Motherwell 0
Celtic 6 Kilmarnock 0
St Johnstone 1 Celtic 2
Hearts 0 Celtic 3
Celtic 1 Rangers 0
Celtic 1 Hibs 1
Dunfermline 0 Celtic 3
Celtic 2 Dundee 1
Aberdeen 0 Celtic 1
Celtic 1 St Mirren 0
Celtic 1 Hearts 0
Rangers 0 Celtic 3
Hibs 2 Celtic 5
Celtic 0 Dundee 2
Kilmarnock 1 Celtic 0

Dundee

Motherwell 0 Dundee 2
Dundee 3 Dunfermline 0
Hibs 5 Dundee 1
Dundee 3 Dundee Utd 0
St Mirren 2 Dundee 1
Dundee 1 Hearts 1
Dundee 1 Rangers 1
St Johnstone 0 Dundee 0
Celtic 1 Dundee 0
Dundee 0 Kilmarnock 0
Aberdeen 0 Dundee 2
Dundee 1 Motherwell 2
Dunfermline 1 Dundee 0
Dundee 0 Hibs 2
Dundee Utd 0 Dundee 2
Dundee 5 St Mirren 0
Hearts 3 Dundee 1
Rangers 2 Dundee 2
Dundee 1 St Johnstone 1
Dundee 1 Celtic 2
Kilmarnock 2 Dundee 3
Dundee 2 Aberdeen 2
Motherwell 0 Dundee 3
Dundee 0 Dunfermline 1
Hibs 3 Dundee 0
Dundee 2 Dundee Utd 3
St Mirren 2 Dundee 1
Dundee 0 Hearts 0
Dundee 0 Rangers 1
St Johnstone 2 Dundee 3
Celtic 2 Dundee 1
Dundee 2 Kilmarnock 2
Aberdeen 0 Dundee 2
Dundee 0 Rangers 3
Dundee 0 Hibs 2
Dundee 2 Kilmarnock 1
Celtic 0 Dundee 2
Hearts 2 Dundee 0

Dundee Utd

Dundee Utd 1 Celtic 2
Hibs 3 Dundee Utd 0
Dundee Utd 1 Motherwell 1
Dundee 3 Dundee Utd 0
Dundee Utd 1 St Johnstone 2
Dunfermline 1 Dundee Utd 0
Kilmarnock 1 Dundee Utd 0
Dundee Utd 0 St Mirren 0
Dundee Utd 3 Aberdeen 5
Rangers 3 Dundee Utd 0
Dundee Utd 0 Hearts 4
Celtic 2 Dundee Utd 1
Dundee Utd 0 Hibs 1
Motherwell 1 Dundee Utd 1
Dundee Utd 0 Dundee 2
St Johnstone 1 Dundee Utd 0
Dundee Utd 3 Dunfermline 2
Dundee Utd 0 Kilmarnock 1
St Mirren 1 Dundee Utd 1
Aberdeen 4 Dundee Utd 1
Dundee Utd 1 Rangers 1
Hearts 3 Dundee Utd 1
Dundee Utd 0 Celtic 4
Hibs 1 Dundee Utd 0
Dundee Utd 2 Motherwell 0
Dundee 2 Dundee Utd 3

THE SCOREBOARD

Home		Away	
Dundee Utd	1	St Johnstone	1
Dunfermline	3	Dundee Utd	1
Kilmarnock	0	Dundee Utd	0
Dundee Utd	4	St Mirren	0
Dundee Utd	1	Aberdeen	1
Rangers	0	Dundee Utd	2
Dundee Utd	1	Hearts	1
St Mirren	2	Dundee Utd	1
Dundee Utd	1	Motherwell	0
Dundee Utd	1	Dunfermline	0
St Johnstone	2	Dundee Utd	3
Aberdeen	1	Dundee Utd	2

Dunfermline

Home		Away	
Dunfermline	0	Aberdeen	0
Dundee	3	Dunfermline	0
Dunfermline	1	St Johnstone	1
Motherwell	0	Dunfermline	1
Rangers	4	Dunfermline	1
Dunfermline	1	Dundee Utd	0
Hearts	2	Dunfermline	1
Dunfermline	1	Celtic	2
Dunfermline	1	Hibs	1
St Mirren	2	Dunfermline	1
Kilmarnock	2	Dunfermline	1
Aberdeen	0	Dunfermline	0
Dunfermline	1	Dundee	0
St Johnstone	0	Dunfermline	2
Dunfermline	1	Motherwell	2
Dunfermline	0	Rangers	0
Dundee Utd	3	Dunfermline	2
Dunfermline	1	Hearts	0
Celtic	3	Dunfermline	1
Hibs	3	Dunfermline	0
Dunfermline	2	St Mirren	0
Dunfermline	1	Kilmarnock	0
Dunfermline	3	Aberdeen	2
Dundee	0	Dunfermline	0
Dunfermline	0	St Johnstone	0
Motherwell	1	Dunfermline	1
Rangers	2	Dunfermline	0
Dunfermline	3	Dundee Utd	1
Hearts	7	Dunfermline	1
Dunfermline	0	Celtic	3
Dunfermline	2	Hibs	1
St Mirren	1	Dunfermline	1
Kilmarnock	2	Dunfermline	1
Aberdeen	1	Dunfermline	0
Dunfermline	1	St Mirren	2
Dundee Utd	1	Dunfermline	1
Dunfermline	1	Motherwell	2
Dunfermline	0	St Johnstone	0

Hearts

Home		Away	
Hearts	0	Hibs	0
St Johnstone	2	Hearts	2
Aberdeen	1	Hearts	1
Hearts	2	St Mirren	0
Hearts	2	Celtic	4
Dundee	1	Hearts	1
Hearts	2	Dunfermline	0
Rangers	1	Hearts	0
Hearts	0	Kilmarnock	2
Hearts	3	Motherwell	0
Dundee Utd	0	Hearts	4
Hibs	6	Hearts	2
Hearts	0	St Johnstone	3
Hearts	3	Aberdeen	0
St Mirren	1	Hearts	2
Celtic	6	Hearts	1
Hearts	3	Dundee	1
Dunfermline	1	Hearts	0
Hearts	0	Rangers	1
Kilmarnock	0	Hearts	3
Motherwell	2	Hearts	0
Hearts	3	Dundee Utd	1
Hearts	1	Hibs	1
St Johnstone	2	Hearts	2
Aberdeen	1	Hearts	0
Hearts	1	St Mirren	2
Hearts	0	Celtic	3
Dundee	0	Hearts	0
Hearts	7	Dunfermline	1
Rangers	2	Hearts	0
Hearts	3	Kilmarnock	0
Hearts	3	Motherwell	0
Dundee Utd	1	Hearts	1
Celtic	1	Hearts	0
Kilmarnock	1	Hearts	1
Hearts	1	Rangers	4
Hibs	0	Hearts	0
Hearts	2	Dundee	0

Hibernian

Home		Away	
Hearts	0	Hibs	0
Hibs	3	Dundee Utd	0
Hibs	5	Hibs	1
Kilmarnock	0	Hibs	1
Aberdeen	0	Hibs	2
Hibs	2	St Mirren	0
Celtic	3	Hibs	0
Hibs	2	Motherwell	0
Dunfermline	1	Hibs	1
St Johnstone	0	Hibs	3
Hibs	1	Rangers	0
Hibs	6	Hearts	2
Dundee Utd	0	Hibs	1
Dundee	1	Hibs	1
Hibs	1	Kilmarnock	1
Hibs	0	Aberdeen	2
St Mirren	1	Hibs	1
Hibs	0	Celtic	0
Motherwell	1	Hibs	3
Hibs	3	Dunfermline	0
Hibs	2	St Johnstone	0
Rangers	1	Hibs	0
Hearts	1	Hibs	1
Hibs	1	Dundee Utd	0
Aberdeen	1	Hibs	0
Hibs	4	St Mirren	2
Celtic	1	Hibs	1
Hibs	1	Motherwell	1
Dunfermline	2	Hibs	1
St Johnstone	2	Hibs	0
Hibs	0	Rangers	0
Hibs	1	Kilmarnock	0
Dundee	1	Hibs	2
Hibs	2	Celtic	5
Hibs	0	Hearts	0
Rangers	4	Hibs	0

Kilmarnock

Home		Away	
St Mirren	0	Kilmarnock	1
Kilmarnock	2	Rangers	4
Celtic	2	Kilmarnock	1
Kilmarnock	0	Hibs	1
Kilmarnock	3	Motherwell	2
St Johnstone	1	Kilmarnock	0
Kilmarnock	1	Dundee Utd	0
Kilmarnock	1	Aberdeen	0
Hearts	0	Kilmarnock	2
Dundee	0	Kilmarnock	0
Kilmarnock	2	Dunfermline	1
Kilmarnock	2	St Mirren	1
Rangers	0	Kilmarnock	0
Kilmarnock	0	Celtic	1
Hibs	1	Kilmarnock	1
Motherwell	1	Kilmarnock	2
Kilmarnock	0	St Johnstone	2
Dundee Utd	0	Kilmarnock	1
Aberdeen	1	Kilmarnock	2
Kilmarnock	0	Dundee	3
Dunfermline	1	Kilmarnock	0
St Mirren	1	Kilmarnock	3
Kilmarnock	1	Rangers	2
Celtic	6	Kilmarnock	0
Kilmarnock	1	Hibs	1
Kilmarnock	1	Motherwell	2
St Johnstone	1	Kilmarnock	2
Kilmarnock	0	Dundee Utd	0
Kilmarnock	0	Aberdeen	0
Hearts	3	Kilmarnock	0
Dundee	2	Kilmarnock	2
Kilmarnock	2	Dunfermline	1
Hibs	1	Kilmarnock	1
Kilmarnock	0	Hearts	1
Dundee	2	Kilmarnock	1
Rangers	5	Kilmarnock	1
Kilmarnock	1	Celtic	0

Motherwell

Home		Away	
Motherwell	0	Dundee	2
Celtic	1	Motherwell	0
Dundee Utd	0	Motherwell	1
Motherwell	0	Dunfermline	1
Kilmarnock	3	Motherwell	2
Motherwell	1	Aberdeen	1
St Mirren	0	Motherwell	1
Hibs	2	Motherwell	0
Motherwell	0	Rangers	1
Hearts	3	Motherwell	0
Motherwell	4	St Johnstone	0
Dundee	1	Motherwell	2
Motherwell	3	Celtic	3
Motherwell	0	Dundee Utd	1
Dunfermline	1	Motherwell	2
Motherwell	1	Kilmarnock	2
Aberdeen	3	Motherwell	3
Motherwell	1	St Mirren	0
Motherwell	1	Hibs	3
Rangers	2	Motherwell	0
Motherwell	1	Hearts	0
Motherwell	0	St Johnstone	1
Dundee Utd	2	Motherwell	0
Motherwell	1	Motherwell	0
Kilmarnock	0	Motherwell	1
Motherwell	0	Aberdeen	1
St Mirren	0	Motherwell	1
Hibs	1	Motherwell	1
Motherwell	1	Rangers	2
Hearts	3	Motherwell	0
Motherwell	1	St Johnstone	0
Motherwell	0	St Johnstone	1
Dundee Utd	1	Motherwell	0
Motherwell	0	Aberdeen	2
Dunfermline	1	Motherwell	2
Motherwell	3	St Mirren	3

Rangers

Home		Away	
Rangers	2	St Johnstone	1
Kilmarnock	2	Rangers	4
St Mirren	0	Rangers	3
Rangers	4	Aberdeen	2
Rangers	4	Dunfermline	1
Celtic	6	Rangers	2
Dundee	1	Rangers	1
Rangers	1	Hearts	0
Motherwell	0	Rangers	1
Rangers	3	Dundee Utd	0
Hibs	1	Rangers	0
St Johnstone	2	Rangers	1
Rangers	0	Kilmarnock	3
Rangers	7	St Mirren	1
Aberdeen	1	Rangers	2
Dunfermline	0	Rangers	0
Rangers	5	Celtic	1
Rangers	0	Dundee	2
Hearts	0	Rangers	1
Rangers	2	Motherwell	0
Dundee Utd	1	Rangers	1
Rangers	1	Hibs	0
Rangers	3	St Johnstone	0
Kilmarnock	0	Rangers	2
St Mirren	1	Rangers	3
Rangers	1	Aberdeen	0
Rangers	2	Dunfermline	0
Celtic	1	Rangers	0
Dundee	0	Rangers	1
Rangers	2	Hearts	0
Motherwell	0	Rangers	2
Rangers	0	Dundee Utd	2
Hibs	0	Rangers	0
Dundee	0	Rangers	3
Rangers	0	Celtic	3

St Johnstone

Home		Away	
Rangers	2	St Johnstone	1
St Johnstone	1	Hearts	2
Dunfermline	1	St Johnstone	1
St Johnstone	0	Celtic	2
Dundee Utd	1	St Johnstone	2
St Johnstone	1	Kilmarnock	1
Aberdeen	1	St Johnstone	1
St Johnstone	0	Dundee	0
St Mirren	0	St Johnstone	1
St Johnstone	0	Hibs	3
Motherwell	4	St Johnstone	0
St Johnstone	2	Rangers	1
Hearts	3	St Johnstone	3
St Johnstone	0	Dunfermline	2
Celtic	4	St Johnstone	1
St Johnstone	1	Dundee Utd	2
Kilmarnock	1	St Johnstone	2
St Johnstone	0	Aberdeen	0
Dundee	1	St Johnstone	1
St Johnstone	2	St Mirren	0
Hibs	2	St Johnstone	0
St Johnstone	2	Motherwell	3
Rangers	3	St Johnstone	0
St Johnstone	2	Hearts	2
Dunfermline	0	St Johnstone	0
St Johnstone	1	Celtic	2
Dundee Utd	1	St Johnstone	1
St Johnstone	1	Kilmarnock	2
Aberdeen	3	St Johnstone	3
St Johnstone	2	Dundee	0
St Mirren	1	St Johnstone	0
St Johnstone	2	Hibs	0
Motherwell	1	St Johnstone	0
St Johnstone	0	Aberdeen	3
St Johnstone	2	St Mirren	2
St Johnstone	2	Dundee Utd	3
Dunfermline	0	St Johnstone	0

St Mirren

Home		Away	
St Mirren	0	Kilmarnock	1
Aberdeen	2	St Mirren	1
St Mirren	1	Rangers	3
Hearts	2	St Mirren	0
St Mirren	2	Dundee	1
Hibs	2	St Mirren	0
St Mirren	0	Motherwell	1
Dundee Utd	0	St Mirren	0
St Mirren	2	Dunfermline	1
Celtic	2	St Mirren	0
Kilmarnock	2	St Mirren	0
St Mirren	2	Aberdeen	0
Rangers	7	St Mirren	1
St Mirren	1	Hearts	2
Dundee	5	St Mirren	0
St Mirren	1	Hibs	1
Motherwell	2	St Mirren	0
St Mirren	1	Dundee Utd	1
St Johnstone	2	St Mirren	0
Dunfermline	2	St Mirren	0
St Mirren	0	Celtic	2
St Mirren	1	Kilmarnock	3
Aberdeen	3	St Mirren	0
St Mirren	1	Rangers	3
Hearts	1	St Mirren	0
St Mirren	2	Dundee	1
Hibs	4	St Mirren	2
St Mirren	0	Motherwell	1
Dundee Utd	4	St Mirren	0
St Mirren	1	St Johnstone	0
St Mirren	1	Dunfermline	1
Celtic	2	St Mirren	0
St Mirren	2	Dundee Utd	1
Dunfermline	1	St Mirren	2
St Johnstone	2	St Mirren	2
St Mirren	2	Aberdeen	1
Motherwell	3	St Mirren	3

SCOTTISH CUP PREVIOUS WINNERS 1950 - 2001					SCOTTISH LEAGUE CUP PREVIOUS WINNERS				
1950–1	Celtic	1	Motherwell	0	1946–7	Rangers	4	Aberdeen	0
1951–2	Motherwell	4	Dundee	0	1947–8	East Fife	4	Falkirk	1
1952–3	Rangers	1	Aberdeen	0	1948–9	Rangers	2	Raith Rovers	0
1953–4	Celtic	2	Aberdeen	1	1949–50	East Fife	3	Dunfermline	0
1954–5	Clyde	1	Celtic	0	1950–1	Motherwell	3	Hibernian	0
1955–6	Hearts	3	Celtic	1	1951–2	Dundee	3	Rangers	2
1956–7	Falkirk	2	Kilmarnock	1	1952–3	Dundee	2	Kilmarnock	0
1957–8	Clyde	1	Hibs	0	1953–4	East Fife	3	Partick Thistle	2
1958–9	St Mirren	3	Aberdeen	1	1954–5	Hearts	4	Motherwell	2
1959–60	Rangers	2	Kilmarnock	0	1955–6	Aberdeen	2	St Mirren	1
1960–1	Dunfermline	2	Celtic	0	1956–7	Celtic	3	Partick Thistle	0
1961–2	Rangers	2	St Mirren	0	1957–8	Celtic	7	Rangers	1
1962–3	Rangers	3	Celtic	0	1958–9	Hearts	5	Partick Thistle	1
1963–4	Rangers	3	Dundee	1	1959–60	Hearts	2	Third Lanark	1
1964–5	Celtic	3	Dunfermline	2	1960–1	Rangers	2	Kilmarnock	0
1965–6	Rangers	1	Celtic	0	1961–2	Rangers	3	Hearts	1
1966–7	Celtic	2	Aberdeen	0	1962–3	Hearts	1	Kilmarnock	0
1967–8	Dunfermline	3	Hearts	1	1963–4	Rangers	5	Morton	0
1968–9	Celtic	4	Rangers	0	1964–5	Rangers	2	Celtic	1
1969–0	Aberdeen	3	Celtic	1	1965–6	Celtic	2	Rangers	1
1970–1	Celtic	2	Rangers	1	1966–7	Celtic	1	Rangers	0
1971–2	Celtic	6	Hibernian	1	1967–8	Celtic	5	Dundee	3
1972–3	Rangers	3	Celtic	2	1968–9	Celtic	6	Hibs	2
1973–4	Celtic	3	Dundee Utd	0	1969–70	Celtic	1	St Johnstone	0
1974–5	Celtic	3	Airdrie	1	1970–1	Rangers	1	Celtic	0
1975–6	Rangers	3	Hearts	1	1971–2	Partick Thistle	4	Celtic	1
1976–7	Celtic	1	Rangers	0	1972–3	Hibs	2	Celtic	1
1977–8	Rangers	2	Aberdeen	1	1973–4	Dundee	1	Celtic	0
1978–9	Rangers	3	Hibernian	2	1974–5	Celtic	6	Hibs	3
1979–80	Celtic	1	Rangers	0	1975–6	Rangers	1	Celtic	0
1980–1	Rangers	4	Dundee Utd	1	1976–7	Aberdeen	2	Celtic	1
1981–2	Aberdeen	4	Rangers	1	1977–8	Celtic	1	Rangers	2
1982–3	Aberdeen	1	Rangers	0	1978–9	Rangers	2	Aberdeen	1
1983–4	Aberdeen	2	Celtic	1	1979–80	Aberdeen	0	Dundee United	3
1984–5	Celtic	2	Dundee Utd	1	1980–1	Dundee	0	Dundee United	3
1985–6	Aberdeen	3	Hearts	0	1981–2	Rangers	2	Dundee United	1
1986–7	St Mirren	1	Dundee Utd	0	1982–3	Celtic	2	Rangers	1
1987–8	Celtic	2	Dundee Utd	1	1983–4	Rangers	3	Celtic	2
1988–9	Celtic	1	Rangers	0	1984–5	Dundee United	0	Rangers	1
1989–90	Aberdeen	0	Celtic	0	1985–6	Aberdeen	3	Hibernian	0
1990–1	Motherwell	4	Dundee Utd	3	1986–7	Celtic	1	Rangers	2
1991–2	Rangers	2	Airdrie	1	1987–8	Rangers	3	Aberdeen	3
1992–3	Rangers	2	Aberdeen	1	1988–9	Aberdeen	2	Rangers	3
1993–4	Dundee Utd	1	Rangers	0	1989–90	Aberdeen	2	Rangers	1
1994–5	Celtic	1	Airdrie	0	1990–1	Rangers	2	Celtic	1
1995–6	Rangers	5	Hearts	1	1991–2	Hibernian	2	Dunfermline	0
1996–9	Kilmarnock	1	Falkirk	0	1992–3	Rangers	2	Aberdeen	1
1997–8	Hearts	2	Rangers	1	1993–4	Rangers	2	Hibernian	1
1998–9	Rangers	1	Celtic	0	1994–5	Celtic	2	Raith Rovers	2
1999–2000	Rangers	4	Aberdeen	0	1995–6	Aberdeen	2	Dundee	0
2000–1	Celtic	3	Hibernian	0	1996–7	Rangers	4	Hearts	3
					1997–8	Celtic	3	Dundee United	0
					1998–9	Rangers	2	St Johnstone	1
					1999–2000	Celtic	2	Aberdeen	0
					2000–1	Celtic	3	Kilmarnock	0